MENG CH'IU

MENG CH'IU

Famous Episodes from Chinese History and Legend

Li Han, Hsü Tzu-kuang

Translated by Burton Watson

KODANSHA INTERNATIONAL LTD.
Tokyo, New York and San Francisco

Library of Congress Cataloging in Publication Data

Li, Han, fl. 746.
  Meng ch'iu: famous episodes from Chinese history and legend.

  Includes index.
  1. Primers, Chinese—Translations into English. 2. Primers—
Translated from Chinese. I. Hsü, Tsu-kuang, 12th cent., joint
author. II. Title. PL 1115.L4614 951'.01 79–89264
ISBN 0–87011–278–3

Distributed in the United States by Kodansha International/
USA Ltd. through Harper & Row, Publishers, Inc., 10 East
53rd Street, New York, New York 10022. In South America by
Harper & Row, International Dept. In Canada by Fitzhenry &
Whiteside Limited, 150 Lesmill Road, Don Mills, Ontario M3B
2T6. In Mexico & Central America by Harla S.A. de C.V.,
Apartado 30–546, Mexico 4, D.F. In the United Kingdom by
Phaidon Press Limited, Littlegate House, St. Ebbe's Street, Ox-
ford OX1 1SQ. In Europe by Boxerbooks, Inc., Limmatstrasse
111, 8031 Zurich. In Australia & New Zealand by Book Wise
(Australia) Pty. Ltd., 104–8 Sussex Street, Sydney 2000. In the
Far East by Toppan Company (S) Pte. Ltd., No. 38 Liu Fang
Road, Jurong, Singapore 2262.

Published by Kodansha International Ltd., 2–12–21 Otowa,
Bunkyo-ku, Tokyo 112 and Kodansha International/USA, Ltd.,
10 East 53rd Street, New York, New York 10022 and 44 Mont-
gomery Street, San Francisco, California 94104. Copyright ©
1979 by Kodansha International Ltd.
All rights reserved. Printed in Japan.

LCC 79–89264
ISBN 0–87011–278–3
JBC 1022–787547–2361

First edition, 1979

CONTENTS

INTRODUCTION

In 746 a Chinese official named Li Liang prepared a memorial to be presented to Emperor Hsüan-tsung of the T'ang dynasty (618–907) in which he recommended to the imperial attention a remarkable book entitled *Meng Ch'iu* by Li Han, a former official in the T'ang bureaucracy. The book, he explained, consisted of historical allusions culled from a wide variety of sources, cast in rhymed form and supplied with notes to explain the events to which they referred. The text was highly suitable for teaching such information to young persons, as evidenced by the amazing erudition of the author's own children, who could recite it by heart. Adults as well, the memorial added, could profit greatly from its perusal.[1]

Because of bureaucratic complications, the memorial was never presented to the throne, and Li Han's textbook had no opportunity to enjoy what no doubt would have been the inestimable boon of an imperial endorsement. Nevertheless, it seems to have gained rapid recognition, and for centuries played a vital role in the education of children in China. Before long, it had also been taken up by the Koreans and Japanese, who were enthusiastic students of Chinese language and culture, and came to exercise a far-reaching influence upon the literatures of those countries as well.

Almost nothing is known of its author Li Han except that he held a minor official post in the early decades of the eighth century. The title of the book, *Meng Ch'iu*, is taken from a passage in the *Book of Changes* (under the hexagram *meng*, #4), which reads: "It is not I who seek out the youthful unenlightened; the youthful unenlightened (*meng*) seek (*ch'iu*) me." Whatever the *Book of Changes* may have meant by this laconic pronouncement, it is clear that Li Han intended the title to convey in elegant and concise form the fact that his book is designed for young people in search of education, though I have been unable to hit upon a suitable English

7

translation that is comparably brief and at the same time intelligible. "Youth Inquires" might be a possibility.

The text of the *Meng Ch'iu* consists of nearly six hundred four-character phrases, each beginning with the name of some person famous in Chinese history or legend followed by two words summing up some action or characteristic for which the person is renowned. The phrases are arranged in pairs marked by neat verbal parallelism, a favorite device in Chinese prose and poetry. The last word of the second phrase in the pair is a rhyme word; a single rhyme is employed four times in succession, after which it gives way to a new rhyme. Thus, for example, the first four pairs of phrases in the book employ the rhyme words *t'ung, hsiung, tung* and *chung*.

Because of this extreme regularity of form and the incorporation of rhyme, the text can be memorized with comparative ease, effectively implanting in the student's mind the names of some six hundred famous personages and an event for which each is remembered. To visualize its nature more clearly, one might imagine a comparable text in English designed for American students that began:

> George Washington chops a cherry,
> Benjamin Franklin flies a kite,
> Betsy Ross sews at midday,
> Paul Revere rides by night. . . .

The demands of parallelism and rhyme were sufficient in themselves to tax the author's ingenuity, and he was not able to present his personages in chronological order. Nor are they limited to any particular period or category, but are drawn from all the dynasties of pre-T'ang history and all walks of life, though persons prominent in political history predominate.

As has often been noted, the Chinese from very ancient times have shown themselves avid readers and writers of history, and the number and volume of historical texts preserved from the nation's past are truly staggering. Moreover, Chinese philosophers and poets have customarily displayed a great fondness for adorning their writings with historical allusions, often cast in the kind of neat parallelisms employed in the *Meng Ch'iu* itself. At an early date it thus became imperative for a person attempting to master the language and literature of China to carry about in his head a vast file of names and anecdotes so that he could quickly identify such allusions and grasp their significance. The Chinese believed that such information could best be instilled in the student by rote memorization, beginning almost in infancy when the mind is particularly adept at such endeavor, leaving the tasks of explanation and analysis to a subsequent period in the student's development. In the earliest centuries of Chinese literary history, entire works were committed to memory, and this continued to be true in later times in the case of texts of particular importance such as the Confucian Classics. But as the mass of historical and philosophical literature continued to swell over the centuries, this approach ceased to be practicable, and digests or encyclopedic works had to be compiled to assist the student in absorbing the mountain of names and facts he was required to know. The *Meng Ch'iu* is an example of one particularly ingenious attempt to solve the student's dilemma, and the enormous popularity it enjoyed in China, Korea, and Japan in the centuries following its appearance is proof that it was an unusually successful one.

As my Americanized *Meng Ch'iu* illustration above will suggest, the four-character phrases of the text are far too cryptic to be understood without considerable background explanation. Li Liang's memorial indicates that the *Meng Ch'iu* was already supplied with notes for that purpose, presumably all or in part the work of the author himself. As the text grew in popularity, other commentators added more elaborate explanations of the incidents and identifications of the sources from which they were drawn, until a variety of editions and commentaries came into circulation and were exported to Korea and Japan along with the basic text. Most of these remained in use until the Southern Sung, when a scholar named Hsü Tzu-kuang in 1189 compiled a new commentary. By his own account he corrected many errors and faulty interpretations that had marred earlier editions and commentaries, and his own edition, probably printed shortly after the date of compilation, rapidly replaced older versions. Many of the earlier commentaries passed out of existence in China and are known only through fragments preserved in Japan or discovered among the manuscripts in the Tun-huang caves of western China. Because later scholars in China and Japan knew only Hsü's commentary, they were at times puzzled by early allusions to the *Meng Ch'iu*. Thus, for example, the famous Japanese woman writer Sei Shōnagon has frequently been accused of somewhat muddling a reference to the *Meng Ch'iu* in her *Pillow Book*; it has since been recognized that she was in fact not muddled at all, but merely following a version of the anecdote recorded in an older commentary, which differed slightly in wording from that found in Hsü's commentary.[2]

The influence which the *Meng Ch'iu* exercised upon Chinese literature during the period of its greatest vogue in the T'ang, Sung and Yuan dynasties was undoubtedly vast, though difficult to pin down, since scholars and writers who may have begun their education with the *Meng Ch'iu* later went on to read and study the texts from which its episodes were drawn. A writer of any pretension, therefore, would take pains to make it appear that his erudition derived from a study of such scholarly works rather than from a children's primer. The drama of the Yuan period, however, presumably because of its more popular nature, draws unabashedly from the text, and *Meng Ch'iu* influence is easily identifiable in many of the plays of the period.

In spite of its wide acceptance, the *Meng Ch'iu* did not escape criticism from certain quarters. According to Confucian views of education, the young should be given moral instruction at the same time they are being fed facts, and it was objected that many of the episodes alluded to in the *Meng Ch'iu* do not present sufficiently exemplary models of behavior. Criticism was also voiced that a number of the episodes dealing with the Three Kingdoms and Chin periods, when Neo-Taoism was in fashion, place too much emphasis upon the teachings of Lao Tzu and Chuang Tzu at the expense of those of Confucius, and otherwise extol eccentric ways of life and thought. Finally, the text was condemned for including stories of the supernatural, since Confucius, the *Analects* tells us, never discoursed on the spirits, and his followers therefore felt compelled to frown on anyone who did. Perhaps as a result of such criticisms, the book in time began to lose favor, at least among the literati, though it probably continued to be utilized on a more popular level. By Ming times (1368–1644) its repute was already on the wane, and in the following Ch'ing period it all but disappeared from sight.

Such, however, was not its fate in Japan, where it is known as the *Mōgyu,* the Sino-Japanese pronunciation of the title. Exactly when it was brought to Japan is uncertain, but in 878 we hear of it being used as a textbook for the education of a prince of the imperial family, the fourth son of Emperor Seiwa. It was apparently employed throughout the Heian period for the instruction of members of the aristocracy, who were at this time expected to have a reading knowledge of Chinese literature. An often-quoted proverb of the period declares that "The sparrows of the Kangaku-in chirp the *Mōgyu.*" The Kangaku-in was a school in Kyoto set up for the education of sons of the powerful Fujiwara clan. The proverb has customarily been interpreted to mean that even the sparrows living in the vicinity of the school have learned the text of the *Mōgyu* by heart, so often have they heard it recited. It is possible, however, that the sparrows are the students themselves, whose piping recitations of the text in Chinese pronunciation would have been as unintelligible to ordinary Japanese ears of the time as the language of the birds. In any event, the text enjoyed a wide readership in Heian upper class society, and unmistakable borrowings from it are found in the *Tale of Genji* and other works of the period.

The edition of the text with Hsü Tzu-kuang's commentary, so popular in China from late Sung times on, probably reached Japan around the beginning of the fourteenth century, though the evidence is uncertain. It is known to have been in use by 1504, and the first edition to be printed in Japan appeared in 1596. As in China, Hsü's version replaced older editions and commentaries, and during the Edo period circulated widely. While the book was gradually sinking into oblivion in the country of its origin, it came to enjoy in Japan in Edo (1603–1867) and early Meiji times (1868–1911) an even greater vogue than in previous centuries. The government in the Edo period actively encouraged the study of Confucianism and the Chinese language, and far more Japanese than ever before took pains to acquire at least an elementary knowledge of Chinese. The *Mōgyu* was ideal for beginners in the language, or for townsmen and lesser samurai who had no serious scholarly ambitions, allowing them to acquire a surprising amount and variety of information with relatively little effort. Many of the most popular writers of the period such as the dramatist Chika-

11

matsu, the fiction writer Saikaku, or the haiku poet Buson, to name only a few, clearly drew the majority of their Chinese allusions from it, which suggests that the audience for which they wrote must also have been conversant with the text. Its four-character phrases were often recast in *senryū*, a light or humorous Japanese verse form resembling the haiku, and many of them passed into the speech of the period. As had been the case earlier in China, the work also inspired a bewildering variety of condensations, continuations, and imitations of various types, among them one in the Meiji period that included personages famous in European and American history along with the Chinese figures of the original. Thus a format conceived in the early eighth century continued to be employed and emulated for over a thousand years after its inception, surely a rare phenomenon in pedagogical literature.

What interest and importance, one may ask, does a textbook written twelve hundred years ago in China have for readers of English today? One answer is immediately forthcoming. If such readers are students of traditional Chinese culture, or of the cultures of countries such as Korea and Japan that were under strong Chinese influence, they must to some extent master the same body of names and facts as the Chinese for whom the book was originally designed. Although no western student of the present day is likely to adopt the old custom of committing the text to memory, he will surely benefit by becoming thoroughly familiar with its contents and keeping it at hand for reference when reading works of Chinese and Japanese literature.

But the *Meng Ch'iu* is of course much more than a mere aid to research. It is a textbook for children, and as such represents what the men and women of traditional China believed it was most important for their young people to learn. In its selection of material it reflects the ideals of the educated class of the period when it was written, and of the succeeding periods when it continued in wide use. One will note first, particularly since most of the episodes are drawn from historical works, the characteristic Chinese emphasis upon history, the imperative to study the past and profit from its lessons. Hsü's commentary meticulously notes the names and birthplace of the subject of each anecdote, reminding one that these are no mere fables or children's stories but accounts of actual

12

events in the nation's history, and subtlely instilling in the youthful reader the hope that he too may someday merit a place in the
annals of his country.

Likewise important as typical of traditional Chinese culture is
the repeated stress upon literature and learning. Though the
Meng Ch'iu includes men who were renowned for their valor or
military exploits, it is the poet and scholar, the official and man of
peaceful accomplishments who loom largest. Nor are women neglected in its pages, the virtuous consort of the ruler, the wise and
frugal housewife figuring prominently among its cast of characters. But, as though to remind the reader that this is not quite the
whole story of Chinese life, and to relieve the prevailing note of
solemnity, the author has inserted here and there an episode illustrative of the more fanciful side of the Chinese temperament,
its love of the witty and paradoxical, the mystical and the bizarre.
It was this very breadth of content, as we have seen, that in time
contributed to the diminution of its popularity. But it is precisely
this variety that makes the text a truer and more comprehensive
mirror of Chinese ideals and attitudes of the past than other works
more narrowly didactic in approach.

Finally the *Meng Ch'iu*, quite apart from its importance as a doc-
ument in the study of Chinese thought and society, commands
attention as a collection of memorable and often highly amusing
anecdotes, anecdotes that are as pertinent to the twentieth century
and the world at large as to the time and place of their origin.
Chinese literature from earliest times is noteworthy for its wealth
of deft and pointed anecdotes. Again and again we find the great
philosophers of antiquity turning to the anecdote rather than
abstract discourse to convey their ideas, and the historian likewise employs the anecdote to sum up the essence and importance
of the personalities he portrays. In the original works of philosophical and historical literature in which they appear, however,
such anecdotes are often embedded within masses of material of a
much drier and more technical nature. The great virtue of the
Meng Ch'iu and its commentary is that they extract these gems
from the voluminous literature that has been handed down and
present them in succinct and highly readable form. Thus, without
plowing through the 100 often wearisome chapters of the *History
of the Former Han* or the 130 chapters of the *History of the Chin*, for

example, the reader can savor some of their most celebrated and engaging passages – and thereafter astound his friends with the breadth of his erudition. No need to tell them, of course, that he acquired his learning by way of the *Meng Ch'iu*.

1. The text of the memorial is included in the prefatory matter to standard editions of the *Meng Ch'iu*.
2. *Makura no sōshi*, sec. 166, the reference to Chu Mai-ch'en. Chu's biography in the *Han shu* or *History of the Former Han* 64A, which Hsü quotes in his commentary, states that Chu told his wife, "By the time I am fifty I will be rich and eminent. Now I am already over forty." But in the old commentary to the *Meng Ch'iu* that Sei Shōnagon evidently knew, the statement reads, "By the time I am forty I will be eminent. I am now thirty-nine." The way Sei Shōnagon alludes to the episode is proof that she drew her knowledge from the *Meng Ch'iu* rather than from the *Han shu*, as some of her admirers would like to believe.

TRANSLATOR'S NOTE

As the basis of my translation I have used the text of the *Meng Ch'iu* and Hsü Tzu-kuang's commentary found in Hayakawa Mitsusaburō, *Mōgyu* (Tokyo: Meiji shoin 1973, 2 vols.). In addition to the Chinese original, notes, and a Japanese translation, this work contains extensive introductory material on the history and importance of the text, its numerous editions, commentaries and imitations, and exhaustive examples of *Meng Ch'iu* influence in Japanese literature.

I have presented here seventy-four couplets from the *Meng Ch'iu* with their accompanying commentary, attempting to select episodes that are particularly well known, illustrative of important themes and attitudes in traditional Chinese literature and culture, and of intrinsic interest because of their wit, pathos, or narrative skill. All are taken from the first half of the text; at some future opportunity I hope to be able to present a similar selection from the latter part of the text. On a few occasions I have expanded the commentary with material taken from the original text upon which it is based in order to make the narrative clearer and more interesting; conversely, I have omitted from the commentary a few passages which are distinctly minor in importance or textual notes of concern only to someone reading the Chinese original.

Where possible, I have supplied dates here and there to give readers not familiar with the epochs of Chinese history some idea of the period in which the events occurred, though I have not attempted to give dates for all the numerous persons mentioned in the text. Dates for emperors and other rulers are those of their reigns.

Early works of Chinese historical and philosophical literature, from which nearly all the episodes in the commentary are drawn, rely heavily upon formulaic language, not because of any poverty of invention, presumably, but out of a desire to convey to the reader the character of a man or the tenor of a period in as concise and elegant form as possible. Economy of expression is in fact one of the most striking characteristics of such works, along with a fondness for direct discourse. Most of the subjects are carefully identified by family, personal, and polite names, and occasionally by official titles and posthumous names as well, along with the subject's birthplace and the dynasty under which he lived, all information considered of vital importance in Chinese historiography.[1] To avoid confusion where a single individual has so many different appellations I have sometimes referred to him in a manner other than that employed in the original. It will also be noted that the author of the *Meng Ch'iu*, in order to fit personal names into his four-character phrase form, has often been obliged to abbreviate them somewhat.

The Finding List at the end of the translation indicates the number of the *Meng Ch'iu* phrase in the Hayakawa text and the source, where known, from which Hsü Tzu-kuang drew his commentary. In customary Chinese fashion, Hsü quotes his source verbatim as far as possible, though at the same time condensing the narrative. As a result, it is not always possible to understand his commentary without reference to the text from which it is abbreviated. Readers who are puzzled as to how I arrived at my translation of any given passage should therefore as a first step consult the original source. For official titles and general manner of treatment I follow the practices adopted in my earlier translations from the *Shih chi* and *Han shu*.

I would like to take this opportunity to express my sincere thanks to Mr. Saburo Nobuki and Kodansha International for making this translation possible.

1. Chinese men customarily have at least two given names, a *ming* or familiar name given in childhood and a *tzu* or polite name given on reaching adulthood. As a mark of humility, a man may refer to himself by his familiar name, but others would ordinarily never address him by anything but his polite name or some other term of address.

SELECTIONS FROM THE MENG CH'IU

1

王戎簡要
WANG JUNG, simple and efficient

裴楷清通
P'EI K'AI, honest and liberal-minded

According to the *History of the Chin*, Wang Jung, whose polite name was Chün-ch'ung, was a native of Lin-i in Lang-ya.[1]

Already in youth he showed remarkable understanding. He was distinguished in appearance and bearing and could stare straight at the sun without being blinded. When P'ei K'ai met him, he looked him over carefully and remarked, "Jung's eyes blaze like flashes of lightning among the cliffs."

Juan Chi was an old friend of Jung's father Wang Hun. When Wang Jung was fifteen he joined his father in the official lodge for palace attendants. Jung was twenty years younger than Juan Chi, but the two struck up a friendship. Whenever Juan Chi had been to visit Wang Hun, he would invariably stop in to see Jung as well, and take leave only after a considerable time. He remarked to Wang Hun, "How honest and praiseworthy your son is – not at all like you. Talking to you can never compare to chatting with young Jung!"

Wang Jung advanced in office until he reached the post of minister of education.

P'ei K'ai of the Chin dynasty, whose polite name was Shu-tse, was a native of Wen-hsi in Ho-tung.

Of keen understanding and copious in knowledge, as a young man he enjoyed a reputation equal to that of Wang Jung. The chancellor Chung Hui recommended him to Emperor Wen, who appointed him a clerk in the office of the chancellor.[2] When a post of gentleman in the board of civil office came vacant, Emperor Wen questioned Chung Hui as to who might fill it. He replied, "Wang Jung is simple and efficient, P'ei K'ai is honest and liberal-minded – either would be suitable for selection." The emperor thereupon appointed P'ei K'ai to the post.

P'ei K'ai was a man of notably superior bearing and handsome appearance. He had browsed widely among books of many varieties, and was particularly versed in the principles of reason.[3] People of the time called him the "jade man." Seeing him, they explained, was like approaching a mountain of jade: he shed a light over and illumined others. He was transferred to the post of gentleman in the office of palace writers. Whenever he entered or left the office, those who chanced to meet him assumed an expression of deference and respect.

When Emperor Wu ascended the throne to found the Chin dynasty [A.D. 265], he divined by the milfoil stalks to see how many generations his rule would last. He was anything but pleased when he received the answer "one," and all the assembled officials turned pale. But P'ei K'ai said, "I have heard that 'Heaven through the virtue of the One is clear, earth through the virtue of the One is stable, and princes and lords through the virtue of the One become upright in the world.' "[4] The emperor was very pleased. P'ei K'ai continued to advance in office until he became chief of palace writers and attendant in the inner palace.

1. The first name is that of the *hsien* or district, the second that of the *chün* or province in which the district is situated; the same applies for similar place names in the episodes that follow.
2. Emperor Wen is the title posthumously bestowed on Ssu-ma Chao, the king of Chin and father of the founder of the Chin dynasty; though he wielded great power, he was never actually emperor.
3. *Li-i*; the term here probably designates in particular the Neo-Taoist philosophy in vogue at this time.
4. P'ei K'ai is quoting from *Lao Tzu* sec. 39; the "One" is the Tao.

2

孔明臥龍

K'UNG-MING, a sleeping dragon

呂望非熊

LÜ SHANG, not a bear ·

According to the *Account of Shu*, Chu-ko Liang, whose polite name was K'ung-ming, was a native of Yang-tu in Lang-ya.

In person he worked the dikes and fields, and liked to recite the "Ballad of Liang-fu."[1] He always used to compare himself to Kuan Chung and Yüeh Yi, but the people of the time refused to go along with this.[2] Only his good friends Ts'ui Chou-p'ing and Hsü Shu believed he was really a match for such men.

When Liu Pei, the first ruler of Shu, was encamped at Hsin-yeh, Hsü Shu went to see him and said, "Chu-ko K'ung-ming is a sleeping dragon. I expect you would like to meet him, would you not? However, he is the kind of man that you may go to visit, but you can never force him to come to visit you. It might be well if you turned your carriage a little out of the way and had a look at him." Liu Pei eventually went to call on Chu-ko Liang, making a total of three visits before he was finally received. Then he took the opportunity to dismiss those around him and to discuss matters of strategy with Chu-ko Liang, and was very pleased with what he heard. Thereafter the two became closer friends with each day that passed.

Kuan Yü, Chang Fei, and Liu Pei's other associates were not pleased, but Liu Pei said, "K'ung-ming means as much to me as water to a fish – you will be good enough to say no more about him!" When Liu Pei declared himself emperor [A.D. 221], he appointed Chu-ko Liang as his chancellor.

The *Liu t'ao* or *Six Bow-cases* records that when King Wen was about to go hunting,[3] his clerk Pien divined with the tortoise shell and announced, "If you hunt on the north side of the Wei River, you will make a great catch – not a dragon, not a hornless dragon, not a tiger, not a brown bear. The signs say you will become a ruler. Heaven is sending you a teacher to give you aid, and it will extend over the reigns of three kings."

21

"But will the signs come true?" asked the king.

Pien replied, "My distant ancestor, the clerk Chou, divined for Emperor Shun when he obtained his eminent minister Kao Yao, and the signs were comparable to these." King Wen thereupon fasted for three days and then went hunting on the north side of the Wei. In time he came upon T'ai-kung (Lü Shang) sitting among the rushes and fishing. King Wen spoke to him comfortingly, questioned him, and in the end placed him in his carriage and returned with him, appointing him as his teacher.

1. A poem in *yüeh-fu* or folk song style dealing with three heroes of the ancient state of Ch'i, in the region where Chu-ko Liang was born. He is usually assumed to be the author of the poem, though there is no evidence to support this.
2. Kuan Chung was an eminent statesman of Ch'i in ancient times, Yüeh Yi a famous general of the neighboring state of Yen.
3. King Wen was the founder, along with his son King Wu and his grandson King Ch'eng, of the Chou dynasty around 1100 B.C. The incident here took place before he had embarked on his campaign to overthrow the Shang dynasty. As predicted, Lü Shang, also known as T'ai-kung Wang, assisted King Wen's son and grandson in founding the dynasty.

匡 衡 鑿 壁

K'UANG HENG bores a hole in the wall

孫 敬 閉 戶

SUN CHING shuts his door

K'uang Heng of the Former Han, whose polite name was Chih-kuei, was a native of Ch'eng in Tung-hai.

His father and his ancestors before him had been farmers, but K'uang took a great liking to learning. However, because his family was poor, he hired himself out as a day laborer in order to meet expenses. In diligence and energy he far surpassed others. The Confucian scholars used to say to each other, "Don't try to lecture on the *Book of Odes* – leave it to K'uang. When he expounds the *Odes*, he makes people laugh so hard they unhinge their jaws!"[1] He passed the civil service examination in the first category and was selected for public office, and in the reign of Emperor Yüan [48–33 B.C.] was promoted to the post of chancellor.

The *Hsi-ching tsa-chi* or *Random Notes on the Western Capital* records that when K'uang Heng was hard at work on his studies, he had no lamp to read by. The house next door had a lamp, but its light did not reach to K'uang's house. K'uang thereupon bored a hole in the wall of his neighbor's house and read his books by the light that came through.

In the village there was a prominent man named Wen Pu-chih, who was very rich and owned many books. K'uang went to work for him, but refused any compensation, asking instead that he be allowed to read his way through the man's library. The master of the rich family, much impressed, kept K'uang provided with books to read, and in this way he was eventually able to become a great scholar.

According to the *Ch'u-kuo hsien-hsien-chuan* or *Biographies of Former Worthies of the State of Ch'u*, Sun Ching, whose polite name was Wen-pao, always kept his door closed and spent all his time reading books. If he felt himself growing drowsy, he would tie a rope around his neck and loop it over the rafters so he would be sure to stay awake. One time when he went to the marketplace, the people in the market, seeing him, all called out, "Here comes Professor Closed Door!" He was invited to take public office but declined the summons.

1. One would like very much to know how he managed to make his lectures on this great anthology of ancient poetry so amusing.

郅 都 蒼 鷹
Chih Tu, the Green Hawk

寧 成 乳 虎
Ning Ch'eng, a nursing tigress

Chih Tu of the Former Han was a native of Ta-yang in Ho-tung.

In the time of Emperor Ching [156–141 B.C.] he was made a general of palace attendants. He had no qualms about voicing his criticisms openly and contradicting the high ministers to their faces at court. Later he was moved to the post of military commander of the capital. At this time the common people were still simple-hearted and ingenuous; they had a genuine fear of breaking the law and took care to stay out of trouble. Chih Tu alone among the officials put sternness and severity above all other qualities, and when it came to applying the letter of the law he made no exception even for the emperor's in-laws. Whenever the feudal lords or members of the imperial family chanced to meet him, they all turned their eyes aside. They nicknamed him "The Green Hawk."

Later Chih Tu was honored with the post of governor of Yen-men Province on the northern border. The Hsiung-nu had long heard of Chih Tu's strict loyalty and integrity, and when he arrived in Yen-men they withdrew their troops from the border; as long as Chih Tu was alive they would not come near the province.[1] The Hsiung-nu leaders even went so far as to fashion a wooden image of Chih Tu and ordered their mounted archers to use it for target practice. So great was the fear he inspired in them, however, that none of them was ever able to hit it. He was a constant source of worry to the Hsiung-nu. Empress Dowager Tou, however, finally managed to find some legal pretext for bringing charges against Chih Tu, and in the end he was executed by being cut in two at the waist.[2]

Ning Ch'eng of the Former Han was a native of Jang in Nan-yang.

He served under Emperor Ching [156–141 B.C.] as a palace

attendant and master of guests. He was a man of great spirit. As long as he was a petty official, he thought of nothing but how he could outdo his superiors, and when he himself became a master of others, he treated the men under him like so much soggy firewood to be summarily bound and bundled into shape. He was appointed military commander of the capital. In restoring order, he imitated the ways of Chih Tu, though he was no match for Chih Tu in integrity.

When Emperor Wu came to the throne, he transferred Ning Ch'eng to the post of prefect of the capital. The emperor's in-laws, however, were assiduous in pointing out Ning Ch'eng's faults and finally managed to have him convicted of some crime. Later the emperor wanted to appoint him to the post of governor of a province. But the imperial secretary Kung-sun Hung said, "When I was still a petty official, Ning Ch'eng was serving as chief commandant of the province of Chi-nan. He governed the people like a wolf rounding up sheep. It would never do to put him in charge of a province!" The emperor ended by assigning him to the post of chief commandant of the Han-ku Pass. After a year of so, the officials of the various provinces and kingdoms to the east who were obliged to go back and forth through the pass were saying, "Better to face a nursing tigress than the wrath of Ning Ch'eng!" Such was his ferocity.

1. The Hsiung-nu were nomadic tribes living in the desert area north of China.
2. Empress Dowager Tou never forgave Chih Tu for hounding her grandson Liu Jung, the king of Lin-chiang, to suicide when the king was summoned to the capital on charges of irregular conduct in 148 B.C.

李 陵 初 詩
Li Ling creates new poems
田 横 感 歌
T'ien Heng inspires sad songs

Li Ling of the Former Han, whose polite name was Shao-ch'ing, was a grandson of the famous general of the vanguard Li Kuang.

As a young man he was made an attendant in the inner palace and supervisor of the Chien-chang Palace. He was good at horsemanship and archery and treated his men well. Modest and deferential, he gave way to others and thereby gained wide fame. Emperor Wu, seeing in him qualities reminiscent of his grandfather Li Kuang, appointed him chief commandant of cavalry. In the second year of the *t'ien-han* era [99 B.C.] he was made commander of a force of five thousand foot soldiers and marched against the Hsiung-nu. He was defeated in battle and eventually surrendered to the enemy.

In his youth, Li Ling had served as a fellow attendant in the inner palace with Su Wu. Later Su Wu was sent as envoy to the Hsiung-nu, and the following year Li Ling surrendered to them. After Emperor Chao came to the throne [86 B.C.], peaceful relations were restored with the Hsiung-nu, and Su Wu, who until that time had been detained by them, was permitted to return to China. Li Ling wrote a poem which he presented to Su Wu on the occasion of his departure:

> *Hand in hand we cross the river bridge –*
> *traveler at twilight, where are you off to?*
> *I linger uncertainly beside the narrow road,*
> *grieving, grieving, unable to say goodby.*
> *The falcon cries in the northern wood,*
> *the firefly wings his way southeast.*
> *Drifting clouds, each day a thousand miles –*
> *how can you know the sorrow in my heart?*

Su Wu in turn composed the following poem of farewell for Li Ling:

Two wild ducks flew north together;
one alone now soars southward.
You must remain here in your lodge,
I must return to my old home.
Once parted, as far apart as Ch'in and Hu;
our time together, how soon it runs out!
Pangs of sorrow tear at my breast;
before I know it, tears stain my robe.
Stay ever in good health, I beg you,
never forget the talk and laughter we had!

The five-character *shih* form began with these poems.[1]

T'ien Heng of the Former Han was a native of Ti and a member of the same T'ien family who had been kings of the state of Ch'i in former times. At the end of the Ch'in dynasty, he set himself up as king of Ch'i [203 B.C.]. The Han general Kuan Ying defeated T'ien Heng's army and eventually gained control of the region of Ch'i. T'ien Heng, fearful of punishment, fled with his followers and took refuge in the islands off the coast. The Han emperor Kao-tsu summoned him to court, whereupon he set off with two of his followers by relay carriage and journeyed to Lo-yang. Apologizing to the imperial envoy who had summoned him, he said, "Once the king of Han and I both faced south and called ourselves sovereign rulers. Now the king of Han has become the Son of Heaven, and I have become a captive fugitive. The shame is too great!" Thereupon he cut his throat, ordering his followers to bear his head and present it to the ruler.

Emperor Kao-tsu wept for him and had him buried with the rites appropriate to a king, at the same time appointing his two followers to the office of chief commandant. After the burial was completed, the two followers scooped out a hole in the side of the grave mound of their lord and slashed their throats. The other five hundred followers who had remained behind in the islands, upon receiving news of T'ien Heng's death, likewise all committed suicide.

Li Chou-han remarks: When T'ien Heng committed suicide, his followers did not dare to lament openly. But their grief was more than they could bear, and therefore they composed a doleful song in order to give vent to their feelings. In later ages it became widely known as the "Dew on the Leek and Graveyard Song," and was used in sending off the dead. The musician Li Yen-nien in time divided it into two works. The "Dew on the Leek" was sung at the funerals of princes, high officials, and noblemen, while the "Graveyard" was sung at the funerals of gentlemen and commoners. The men who pulled the coffin along would sing the songs, and hence they came to be known as *wan-ko* or "coffin-pullers' songs."[2]

1. These and similar poems attributed to Li Ling and Su Wu, long regarded as genuine, were thought to be the earliest examples of poetry in the five-character *shih* form; scholars now believe them to be of considerably later date, probably around A.D. 200.
2. The closing passage by the T'ang commentator on the *Wen hsüan* Li Chou-han is taken from his note on the "coffin-pullers' songs" in *Wen hsüan* 28. The two songs attributed to T'ien Heng's followers, which appear to be genuine Han works, read as follows:

> *Dew on the leek,*
> *how quickly it dries!*
> *Dew that dries*
> *will fall again tomorrow morning,*
> *but a man once gone away in death,*
> *when will he return?*
>
> *The graveyard — who makes his home in that land?*
> *Gathered ghosts, wise and foolish alike.*
> *Lord of spirits, why must you hurry us so!*
> *Man's life allows not a moment of lingering.*

6

武 仲 不 休

WU-CHUNG never gives up

士 衡 患 多

SHIH-HENG worries about having too much

Fu Yi of the Later Han, whose polite name was Wu-chung, was a native of Mou-ling in Fu-feng.

In his youth he was noted for his broad learning, and when Emperor Chang [A.D. 76–88] was searching far and wide for men of literary ability to summon to his court, he selected Fu Yi to be a chief clerk of the Orchid Terrace library, at the same time appointing him a palace attendant. Fu Yi worked with Pan Ku and Chia K'uei in supervising the collating of texts. He was very voluble in praising the virtues of the deceased Emperor Ming, Emperor Chang's father.

At that time, no hymns had as yet been composed for use in Emperor Ming's funerary temple. Fu Yi, using as a model the "Pure Temple" poem in the *Book of Odes*,[1] thereupon composed ten hymns to Emperor Ming which he presented to the throne. As a result, he became renowned at court for his literary excellence. The *Lun wen* or "Essay on Literature" by Emperor Wen of the Wei dynasty states: From past times it has always been the custom for literary men to disparage one another. Fu Yi was like a brother to Pan Ku in terms of literary talent, and yet Pan Ku insisted upon belittling him. In a letter to his young brother Pan Ch'ao, Pan Ku remarked, "Fu Wu-chung because of his ability in composition was made a chief clerk in the Orchid Terrace. But once he picked up his writing brush he never seemed to know when to give up!"

Lu Chi of the Chin dynasty, whose polite name was Shih-heng, was a native of the former state of Wu and a son of the grand marshal Lu K'ang. He was seven feet tall and had a voice like a bell.[2] In his youth he displayed unusual talent and in literary ability was the leader of his time.

After the state of Wu had been overthrown [A.D. 277], Lu Chi and his younger brother Lu Yün together entered the Chin capital at Lo-yang and called on the master of ritual Chang Hua. Chang Hua had long admired their reputation and treated them like old friends, remarking, "In our campaign against the state of Wu, our greatest prize has been the acquisition of you two fine men!"

They also visited the attendant of the inner palace Wang Chi. Wang Chi, pointing to a beverage made of fermented sheep's milk, said, "I doubt that you have anything in Wu that can compare to this."

Lu Chi replied, "It's something like our famous water shield soup of Ch'ien-li, only without the proper sauce to go with it." The people of the time all admired him for such an apt answer.[3]

Lu Chi was a man of extraordinary genius and his writings were marked by great breadth and beauty. Chang Hua once said to him, "Other people when they write always regret that they have so little talent, but in your case you have to worry about having too much!" And in a letter to his older brother, Lu Yün once remarked, "When I look at your writings, I always feel like burning my writing brushes and inkstone."

Chang Hua recommended Lu Chi to the other high officials, and he was employed and promoted until he reached the post of gentleman in the office of palace writers. Later, when Ssu-ma Ying, the prince of Ch'eng-tu, called out his troops and attacked Ssu-ma Yi, the prince of Ch'ang-sha, he assigned Lu Chi to a temporary appointment as general of the rear and military governor of Ho-pei. But Lu Chi was a stranger from the south and, having entered official service, was now suddenly raised to a position superior to that of the other officials. As a result, they all hated him and slandered him to Ssu-ma Ying. Ssu-ma Ying, infuriated, sent men to arrest him. Lu Chi said with a sigh, "The storks of Hua-ting back home in Wu – when will I ever hear their cries again?" Eventually he was put to death.[4]

When Lu Chi was young he had a very clever dog named Yellow Ears. When he went north and was living in the capital at Lo-yang, he had had no news from home for a long time and he said to his dog with a laugh, "I don't seem to get any letters from home. Do you think you could deliver a letter for me and bring back the answer?" The dog wagged his tail and barked. Lu Chi thereupon wrote a letter, stuffed it into a bamboo tube, and tied the tube to the dog's neck. The dog then took to the road, bounding off toward the south, and eventually reached Lu Chi's home, where he was given an answer and returned with it to Lo-yang. After this, he went back and forth any number of times with letters.

1. Mao text #266.
2. The Chinese foot was about three fourths of the English foot.
3. An early example of the bickering that went on between northern and southern Chinese regarding the relative merits of their respective regions.
4. In A.D. 303. Lu Chi's best known work is the *Wen fu* or "Rhyme-prose on Literature," a long poem of great beauty that constitutes one of the earliest and most important statements on Chinese literary theory.

7

劇 孟 一 敵
CHÜ MENG worth one of the enemy states

周 處 三 害
CHOU CH'U and the three plagues

Chü Meng of the Former Han was a native of Lo-yang and was
famous for his deeds of chivalry. When the states of Wu and
Ch'u began their revolt [154 B.C.], Chou Ya-fu, the marquis of
T'iao, was made grand commandant of the Han armies and hastened east to Ho-nan, where he met Chü Meng. He was delighted
and said, "Wu and Ch'u have embarked on a very serious under-
taking, but since they have not sought your services, I am sure
they will not be able to accomplish anything!" By this he meant
that, at a time when the whole empire was in turmoil, the support
of Chü Meng was worth more to him than the conquest of one of
the rebel kingdoms.

Chou Ch'u of the Chin, whose polite name was Tzu-yin, was
a native of Yang-hsien in I-hsing.

In strength of limb he far exceeded others, and since he did not
bother with the niceties of conduct, he was a source of great
worry to the community. He himself was aware that people hated
him, and resolutely made up his mind to reform his ways. He
said to the elders of the village, "Now the times are peaceful and
the harvest is good. Why do you look so distressed instead of enjoying yourselves?"

The elders replied with a sigh, "Until the three plagues have
been done away with, how can there be any joy?"

"What are the three plagues?" asked Chou Ch'u.

They replied, "The fierce tiger with the white forehead in
Southern Mountain, the hornless dragon that lives under Long
Bridge – and you're the third!"

"I can get rid of them for you!" said Chou Ch'u. Then he went
to the mountain and with his bow felled the fierce tiger. He dived
into the water and beat the hornless dragon to death. And in due
time he reformed his ways, developed a taste for learning, and
became a man of refined mind. He was righteous and impassioned

in action and loyal and trustworthy in word. After a year spent in self-discipline, he was selected for one post after another in the local government. He became an official of the Chin and was appointed middle aide to the imperial secretary. When he was called upon to investigate or impeach someone, he did not hesitate even if the person happened to be a relative or favorite of the ruler.

When Ch'i Wan-nien, a leader of the Ti tribes, raised his revolt [A.D. 296], the court officials, angered at Chou Ch'u because of his outright and forceful ways, all declared, "Chou Ch'u is the son of a famous general and a man of loyalty and integrity!" The emperor thereupon placed him under the command of Hsia-hou Chün and sent him off on the expedition to the west. The General Who Calms the Waves Sun Hsiu said to him, "You have an elderly mother. You can get out of the assignment on that account if you wish."

But Chou Ch'u replied, "How can one hope to fulfill the requirements of fidelity to one's lord and filial piety both at once? I took leave of my parents when I entered the service of the ruler. They can't expect me to go on acting like a son!"

He engaged the enemy troops and suffered defeat, whereupon those around him urged him to retreat. But Chou Ch'u gripped the hilt of his sword and replied, "Today is the day when I prove my loyalty and carry out my orders – what is this talk of retreat? In past times when a general received his orders he departed by the northern gate, the gate of death. It signified that he could advance, but never retreat. Now if you gentlemen betray your trust, we will never be able to regain the advantage. I am a high official. Is it not right that I should lay down my life for my country?" Thus he continued to fight with all his strength until he was slain. He was awarded the posthumous title of General Who Pacifies the West.

8

墨子悲絲
Mo Tzu grieves for the silk

楊朱泣岐
Yang Tzu weeps at the crossroads

The *Huai-nan Tzu* says: The philosopher Yang Tzu would weep when he saw a crossroads, thinking how one could go either north or south. The philosopher Mo Tzu shed tears when he saw a skein of raw silk, thinking how it could be dyed either yellow or black.

Kao Yu, the commentator on the *Huai-nan Tzu*, says: They sorrowed that things should be the same at the start but so different in the end.

9

杜后生齒
Empress Tu grows a set of teeth
靈王出髭
King Ling is born with a moustache

According to the *History of the Chin*, Empress Tu (known post-humously as Kung or Ling-yang), the consort of Emperor Ch'eng [A.D. 326–42], was a great-granddaughter of the Chen-nan general Tu Yü. From the time she was a child she was very beautiful to look at, but even after reaching maturity she never developed any teeth. As a result, when marriage proposals came her way, the negotiations invariably broke off in the middle. But when Emperor Ch'eng sent his betrothal gifts and requested her hand, she grew a complete set of teeth in a single night. She occupied the position of empress for six years but had no children.

Sometime earlier, some girls of the region of Three Wu were seen adorning one another's hair with white flowers that from a distance looked like white crab-apple blossoms. The rumor got around that the Weaving Maiden of Heaven had died and that the girls were donning mourning for her.[1] It was just at this time that Empress Tu passed away.

According to the *Tso Chuan*, Prince Chao of the Chou dynasty said, "In the sixth year of King Ting [601 B.C.], the men of Ch'in handed down a weird prophecy, proclaiming that the house of Chou would have a moustached king who was highly capable in the execution of his duties. The feudal lords would acknowledge his authority and send in their tribute, and for the reigns of two kings, they would fulfill their duties. After that, there would be plots to seize the throne, and if the feudal lords did not take heed, they would suffer in the ensuing rebellion and disorder.

"Later, King Ling, the grandson of King Ting, was born with a moustache. He was a very wise and holy ruler and aroused no animosity among the feudal lords. Both he and his successor King Ching lived out their reigns in peace."

1. The Weaving Maiden is a constellation centering around Vega. In Chinese custom white is the color of mourning.

36

賈誼忌鵩
CHIA YI dreads the owl

莊周畏犧
CHUANG CHOU shudders at the sacrificial ox

Chia Yi of the Former Han was a native of Lo-yang. By the age of eighteen he was already renowned in his province for his ability to recite the *Book of Odes* and *Book of Documents* and to compose works of literature. Lord Wu, the governor of Ho-nan, heard of his outstanding ability and invited him to be one of his retainers. Later, when Lord Wu became commandant of justice, he reported to Emperor Wen [179–157 B.C.] that Chia Yi, though still young, had fully mastered the writings of the hundred schools of philosophy.

The emperor accordingly summoned Chia Yi and made him an erudite. Whenever the draft of some edict or ordinance was referred to the scholars for discussion, though the older masters might be unable to say a word, Chia Yi would give a full reply, expressing what each of the others would like to have said. The other scholars regarded him as a man of ability and the emperor, pleased with him, advanced him with unusual rapidity, so that in the space of a year he reached the position of palace counselor.

Chia Yi believed that a sufficient time had elapsed since the founding of the dynasty and that the Han should alter the month upon which the year began, change the color of the vestments and other details of procedure, fix the titles of officials, and encourage the spread of rites and music. He drew up a draft of his proposals on matters of ceremony, but the emperor modestly denied any ability or leisure to put them into effect. The changes that were later made in the laws and regulations, however, were all initially suggested by Chia Yi.

The emperor wanted to promote Chia Yi to one of the high ministerial posts in the government, but Chou P'o, Kuan Ying, and the rest of their group all disparaged him. After this the emperor too grew cold toward Chia Yi and ceased to listen to his proposals, instead appointing him as grand tutor to the king of Ch'ang-sha. Three years later, a *fu* one day flew into Chia Yi's lodge and perched on the corner of his mat. A *fu* is a kind of owl and is a bird of ill omen. At that time Chia Yi had been disgraced and sent to live in Ch'ang-sha, a damp, low-lying region. He was filled with horror and grief by the event, believing that he did not have long to live. Thereupon he composed a poem in the rhyme-prose form to console himself.[1]

A year or so later, the emperor remembered Chia Yi and re-called him to the capital. When Chia Yi went in for an audience with the emperor, the latter was seated in the Great Hall receiv-ing the sacrificial meats from the various shrines, and his mind was accordingly filled with thoughts of the gods and spirits. He questioned Chia Yi about the true nature of spiritual beings, and Chia Yi explained the matter to him in great detail, talking far into the night while the emperor leaned forward on his mat in rapt attention. After the emperor had dismissed Chia Yi, he said, "I have not seen Master Chia for a long time. I used to think I knew more than he, but now I see I am no match for him!" After this, he appointed Chia Yi as grand tutor to the king of Liang. Chia Yi died at the age of thirty-three. K'ung Tsang in his own "Rhyme-prose on the Owl" wrote:

> *Master Chia, learned man of the past,*
> *knew enough to dread the owl.*

The *Chuang Tzu* says: Someone sent gifts to Chuang Tzu with an invitation to office. Chuang Tzu replied to the messenger in these words: "Have you ever seen a sacrificial ox? They deck him out in embroidery and trimmings, gorge him on grass and beanstalks. But when at last they lead him off into the great an-cestral temple, then, although he might wish he could become a lonely calf once more, is it possible?"

The *Shih chi* or *Records of the Historian* records that Chuang Chou was a native of Meng and once served as an official in the lacquer garden of Meng. He was a contemporary of King Hui of Liang [370–319 B.C.]. His doctrines are based on those of Lao Tzu. He wrote a book that is mostly in the nature of fable, broad and bold in expression and stressing freedom and the satisfaction of the self. For that reason the rulers and high officials of the time were unable to find any application for it. King Wei of Ch'u, having heard that Chuang Chou was a worthy man, dispatched a messenger with generous gifts to invite him to take office, even promising to make him prime minister. Therefore Chuang Chou spoke the words quoted above in declining the invitation. Kuo Hsiang, the commentator on the *Chuang Tzu*, remarks, "He who delights in life will shudder at the sacrificial ox and decline the gifts."

1. The poem, written in 174 or 173 B.C., is translated in my *Chinese Rhyme-prose: Poems in the Fu Form from the Han and Six Dynasties Periods*, (New York: Columbia University Press 1971), pp. 25–28.

11

燕昭築臺
King Chao of Yen builds a terrace

鄭莊置驛
Cheng Chuang stations post horses

According to the *Shih chi* or *Records of the Historian,* when King
Chao of Yen [311–279 B.C.] came to the throne, he humbled himself and treated others generously in order to attract worthy men
to his service. He said to Kuo Wei, "The state of Ch'i took advantage of the confusion in my father's time to attack and defeat us. I am only too well aware that Yen is a small and powerless
state and can never hope to exact revenge. But if I could only get
worthy men to help me in my rule and somehow wipe out the disgrace that my father the former king suffered, that would be my
greatest desire. If you would be good enough to point out such men
to me, I could see that they are treated with the proper courtesy."

Kuo Wei replied, "If Your Majesty really wishes to attract
gentlemen, you should start by treating me well. Then others who
are far more worthy that I will think nothing of journeying here
from a thousand miles away!"

King Chao thereupon built a special residence for Kuo Wei
and treated him as his teacher. Before long Yüeh Yi arrived from
Wei, Tsou Yen from Ch'i, Chü Hsin from Chao – men of worth
were scrambling over each other in their haste to move to Yen.
After this, Yen joined with Ch'in, Ch'u, Han, Wei, and Chao in
plotting an attack on Ch'i. Ch'i was defeated, and the only cities
that did not fall to the invaders were Liao, Chü, and Chi-mo;
all the rest surrendered to Yen.

K'ung Jung in his famous letter to Ts'ao Ts'ao says, "King
Chao built a terrace to show respect for Kuo Wei." And a poem
in *yüeh-fu* or ballad form by Pao Chao contains these lines:

> *Was it only gifts of white jade he offered?*
> *He would build a yellow gold terrace too.*

A note on this explains that King Chao of Yen placed a thousand
pieces of gold on top of the terrace in order to attract the finest
men from all over the empire.

Cheng Tang-shih of the Former Han, whose polite name was Chuang, was a native of Ch'en.

During the reign of Emperor Wen he amused himself by performing daring exploits. After he succeeded in rescuing the general Chang Yü of Liang from difficulty, he achieved considerable fame in the area of Liang and Ch'u. In Emperor Ching's time he was made a retainer in the household of the heir apparent. Every five days, when his bath and hair-washing day came around,[1] he would have post horses stationed in the suburbs of Ch'ang-an for the convenience of the guests whom he would invite to his home. He would feast them far into the night, his constant fear being that he would not get around to entertaining them all. The people he associated with were all of his grandfather's generation and included some of the most famous men of the empire. In Emperor Wu's reign [140–87 B.C.] he advanced to the post of minister of agriculture.

While he was acting as a high official, he cautioned his gate-keeper that, whenever visitors came to the house, regardless of whether they were of high rank or low, they were not to be kept waiting at the gate but were to be shown in with all due courtesy. This was the way that Cheng Chuang, in spite of his high position, humbled himself before others. He also worked to boost his subordinate officials and assistants into higher positions by constantly declaring that they were more worthy than himself. If he heard of some worthwhile suggestion that someone else had made, his only thought was to report it to the emperor as quickly as possible. For this reason, gentlemen and men of prominence from east of the mountains all joined together in praising him. Later he became implicated in an offense committed by someone else, but was eventually restored to office and died in the post of governor of Ju-nan. He left no excessive accumulation of wealth to his family.

Sometime earlier, there was a man named Lord Ti of Hsia-kuei who held the office of commandant of justice. At that time he had so many guests that they completely filled his gate. Later, however, when he lost his position, he might have spread a sparrow net in front of his gate without fear of anyone stumbling into it. In time he was restored to the post of commandant of justice and all his old visitors wanted to come to see him again, but Lord

41

Ti wrote in large letters over the top of his gate the following inscription:

"One dead, one alive – then you know how deep their friendship was.

"One rich, one poor – then you know the quality of their friendship.

"One eminent, one lowly – then you can see what friendship means to them."[2]

1. The periodic holiday of court officials, when they were allowed to leave the palace and return to their homes to "bathe and wash their hair."
2. The last section on Lord Ti is taken from the concluding remarks which Ssu-ma Ch'ien appended to his biographies of Cheng Chuang and Chi An in *Shih chi* 120. Both men were deserted by their friends when they lost their former high positions.

12

瓘 靖 二 妙

KUAN and CHING, two wonders

岳 湛 連 璧

YÜEH and CHAN, a pair of jewels

According to the *History of the Chin*, Wei Kuan, whose polite name was Po-yü, was a native of An-i in Ho-tung.

In the reign of Emperor Wu [A.D. 265–90] he was appointed chief of palace writers, and at the same time was made an attendant in the inner palace. He was by nature very stern and correct and dealt with those under him in strict accordance with the law. Clerks in his office were treated like ordinary underlings and even the higher officials under him were shown no special preference.

Wei Kuan was a man of wide learning and demonstrated great appreciation and skill in the arts. He and one of the gentlemen in the office of palace writers named So Ching were both proficient at writing in grass script and people of the time referred to them as the "Two Wonders in One Office." At the end of the Han dynasty there had been a man named Chang Chih who was also highly skilled in grass script. Connoisseurs of calligraphy used to say, "Wei Kuan has got Chang Chih's sinew and So Ching has got his flesh." Wei Kuan could handle the brush better than So Ching, but he could not begin to equal the latter in his grasp of the principles of proper calligraphy.

So Ching, whose polite name was Yu-an, was a native of Tun-huang.

In youth his abilities outshone those of the other men of the district and he joined Fan Chung, Chang Piao, So Chi, and So Yung, also from Tun-huang, in journeying to the capital to enter the government university. Their fame spread throughout the area within the four seas and they were known as the "Five Dragons of Tun-huang." So Ching was widely versed in the Classics and histories, was recommended as a man of "worth and goodness," and passed the civil service examination in the highest category. He was advanced in office until he reached the post of scouting and attacking general.

P'an Yüeh of the Chin dynasty, whose polite name was An-jen, was a native of Chung-mou in Ying-yang.

In youth he won praise for his exceptional talent and was dubbed by the people of his region "the boy wonder." It was said that he belonged in a class with Chung Chün and Chia Yi of the Former Han, who were also famous for their precocious brilliance.

Hsia-hou Chan, whose polite name was Hsiao-jo, was a native of Ch'iao in Ch'iao-kuo. He was a talented young man who wrote in a rich and varied style and was particularly good at coining new phrases. He was very handsome and was a close friend of P'an Yüeh. They would always ride around in the same carriage or sit side by side on the same mat, so that the people of the capital came to speak of them as a "pair of jewels." This was because P'an Yüeh likewise was extremely good looking and commanded a literary style of superlative beauty.

In his youth P'an Yüeh would frequently tuck his crossbow beneath his arm and ride off on the roads of Lo-yang. At such times the women who encountered him would all join hands and crowd around his carriage, throwing him presents of fruit, until he would return home with a carriage full of fruit. He was chosen for government service as a man of "outstanding talent," and in fame outshone his contemporaries, but because so many people were jealous and resentful of him, he remained idle and unemployed for ten years. He was finally dispatched to the post of magistrate of Ho-yang, but he had a very high opinion of his ability and was disgruntled that the post was not more to his liking. Later he advanced to the rank of attendant of the Yellow Gate in the imperial palace.

Meanwhile, Hsia-hou Chan was recommended as a man of "worth and goodness" and passed the civil service examination in the middle category. He reached the post of gentleman in constant attendance and supplementary cavalryman.[1]

1. P'an Yüeh's checkered career ended in A.D. 300 when he was accused by a disgruntled rival and executed on charges of treason; Hsia-hou Chan died around 291.

13

邵 詵 一 枝

Hsi Shen, a single branch

戴 憑 重 席

Tai P'ing, multiple mats

According to the *History of the Chin*, Hsi Shen, whose polite name was Kuang-chi, was a native of Tan-fu in Chi-yin.

Of broad learning and manifold talent, he was a highly unusual and strongminded man who did not allow himself to be bound by petty rules of conduct. Though politely invited by both the local and district authorities to take office, he declined all offers. During the *t'ai-shih* era [A.D. 265–74] he was recommended as a man of "worth and goodness," passed the civil service examination in the highest category, and was appointed a palace attendant in charge of deliberations. Later he was assigned to the post of provincial director of Yung-chou. When Emperor Wu assembled the various new appointees in the Eastern Hall to send them off to their assignments, he asked Hsi Shen, "What do you think of your accomplishments?"

Hsi Shen replied, "I was selected as a man of 'worth and goodness' and on the examination received the highest grade in the empire. Yet what I have won is only a single branch of the cassia forest, a fragment of jade among the riches of the K'un-lun Mountains."[1] The emperor laughed. In office Hsi Shen displayed great strictness of conduct and wisdom in decision, and for these qualities won the highest praise.

Tai P'ing of the Later Han, whose polite name was Tz'u-chung, was a native of P'ing-yü in Ju-nan.

In the time of Emperor Kuang-wu [A.D. 25–57] he was recommended as an "expert in the Classics" and took the examination for the post of erudite. Later he was appointed an attendant in the inner palace. On the first day of the year, when the hundred officials had gathered at the morning audience to pay their respects to the emperor, the emperor gave orders that all those ministers who were capable of expounding the Classics should challenge each other with difficult questions. Those whose explanations were unsatisfactory were to have their sitting mats taken away from them, the mats to be given to those whose answers were deemed correct. As a result, Tai P'ing ended up sitting on a pile of over fifty mats. Because of this incident, the people in the capital used to say:

Attendant in the inner palace Tai –
expounding the Classics, never stuck for a reply!

1. From this remark derives the expression *che-kuei*, "to pluck the cassia," meaning to pass the civil service examination.

晉宣狼顧
EMPEROR HSÜAN of the Chin, a wolf's glance

14

漢祖龍顏
KAO-TSU of the Han, a dragon countenance

Emperor Hsüan of the Chin dynasty, whose personal name was Yi and whose polite name was Chung-ta, was a native of the village of Hsiao-ching in Wen district in Ho-nei. His family name was Ssu-ma.[1]

As a youth he was very bright and full of great plans, well-read and broad in knowledge. During the terrible chaos at the end of the Later Han, he was troubled at heart and constantly pondered over the ills of the empire. When Ts'ao Ts'ao was prime minister of the Han, Ssu-ma Yi was appointed clerk to the men of learning, and later advanced step by step until he himself became prime minister under the Wei dynasty. His grandson Ssu-ma Yen became the first emperor of the Chin dynasty, the throne having been ceded to him by Emperor Yüan of the Wei. At that time Ssu-ma Yen honored his grandfather by bestowing upon him the honorary title of Emperor Hsüan.

Ssu-ma Yi was at heart a harsh man, though outwardly he gave the impression of being easygoing. He was wary and suspicious and full of schemes for power. Ts'ao Ts'ao observed him closely and knew that he had great and far-reaching ambitions. He had also heard that Ssu-ma Yi had a habit of glancing behind him like a wolf and decided to test him. He therefore summoned Ssu-ma Yi into his presence, ordered him to walk forward, and then called to him to look back. Ssu-ma Yi did so, but at the same time kept the rest of his body motionless, facing forward.

Ts'ao Ts'ao also once dreamt of three horses eating out of a single trough and was filled with loathing by the dream.[2] He accordingly said to his son and heir Ts'ao P'ei, "Ssu-ma Yi will not remain a subject forever. Someday you are bound to find him taking over your family affairs from you!" Ts'ao P'ei, however, had always been on good terms with Ssu-ma Yi and the two aided and protected each other. As a result, Ts'ao P'ei was able to reign without mishap.

47

Emperor Kao-tsu of the Former Han, whose personal name was Pang and whose polite name was Chi, was a native of the village of Chung-yang in the township of Feng in P'ei. His family name was Liu.

His mother was one day resting on the bank of a large pond when she dreamed that she encountered a god. At that time the sky grew dark and was filled with thunder and lightning. When Kao-tsu's father went to look for her, he saw a scaly dragon over the place where she was lying. After this she became pregnant and in time gave birth to Kao-tsu. He had a prominent nose and a dragon countenance, with beautiful whiskers on his chin and cheeks; on his left thigh he had seventy-two black moles. He was generous, kind, and affectionate with others, and very broad and understanding in mind. He always had great plans and paid little attention to the business the rest of his family was engaged in.[3]

1. As will be seen, Ssu-ma Yi never actually ruled, but gradually usurped power from the Ts'ao family, rulers of the Wei dynasty (A.D. 220–64), thus making it possible for his grandson Ssu-ma Yen to overthrow the Wei in 265 and found a dynasty of his own called the Chin.
2. The surname Ssu-ma contains the word for horse, and the three horses thus represent Ssu-ma Yi, his son Ssu-ma Chao, and his grandson Ssu-ma Yen. The word for "trough" is a homophone for the surname Ts'ao. The dream portends the overthrow of the Ts'ao family by the Ssu-ma.
3. He was a leader in the revolt that overthrew the Ch'in dynasty and in 206 B.C. founded the Han.

15

鮑 靚 記 井
Pao Ching recalls a well

羊 祜 識 環
Yang Hu remembers a ring

According to the *History of the Chin*, Pao Ching, whose polite name was T'ai-hsüan, was a native of Tung-hai.

When he was five years old, he said to his father and mother, "I was originally the son of the Li family of Ch'ü-yang. At the age of nine I fell into a well and died." When his father and mother made inquiries, they found that everything he had said tallied with the facts. Pao Ching studied both the inner learning of Taoism and the outer learning of Confucianism, and was particularly versed in astronomy and the books of the Yellow River and the Lo.[1] Later he was appointed governor of Nan-hai. He once met an immortal spirit named the Dark Lord who taught him the secrets of the Tao. He lived to be over a hundred.

Yang Hu of the Chin dynasty, whose polite name was Shu-tzu, was a native of Nan-ch'eng in T'ai-shan.

His family had for generations been local officials of the two-thousand-picul class. Yang Hu represented the ninth generation, and all had been known for their honesty and virtue. When Yang Hu was five years old, he told his wet nurse to bring him the gold ring he always played with. The nurse replied, "You never had any such thing in the past!" Yang Hu then went at once to the Li family next door, searched about the mulberry tree that grew by the east hedge, and came up with a gold ring.

The master of the house exclaimed in surprise, "This is the ring my dead boy lost! What are *you* doing with it!" The nurse then explained to him what Yang Hu had said. Mr. Li was overwhelmed with grief. The people of the time, wondering at the incident, said that Yang Hu in a former life must have been Mr. Li's son.

Yang Hu became a highly learned man and was good at writing. In the time of Ts'ao Mao of the Wei, the Duke of Kao-kuei-hsiang, Yang Hu was summoned to the office of public carriage and was appointed gentleman in attendance in the office of palace writers. When Emperor Wu [A.D. 265–89] of the Chin decided to launch a campaign to wipe out the state of Wu, he made Yang Hu the supervisor of military affairs in Ching-chou. Yang Hu took part in the campaign and gained control of the area of Nan-hsia. Later he advanced to the rank of General Who Conquers the South and was enfoeffed as marquis of Nan-ch'eng. After his death he was posthumously awarded the title of grand tutor.

Earlier, a man who was skilled in examining grave sites and predicting the fortunes of the family had said that the grave of Yang Hu's ancestors showed signs indicating the appearance of an emperor or a king, but that if the grave were bored into, the family would be cut off without posterity. Later Yang Hu, fearful of arousing the ire of the ruling family, had the grave bored into. The diviner of graves, observing this, said, "The family will still produce a man with a broken arm who will hold one of the three highest ministerial posts!" Eventually, Yang Hu fell off his horse and broke his arm, became one of the three highest ministers, but left no heir.

Yang Hu loved the mountains and waters, and whenever the weather was fine, he would invariably pay a visit to Mount Hsien. Setting out wine, he would compose poems and spend all day there without growing weary. The common people of Hsiang-yang set up a stele at the place where Yang Hu had customarily held his outings and established a funerary temple in which they presented offerings to him at each season of the year. Gazing at the stele, there was none who did not shed tears. For this reason Tu Yü named it the "Stele of Fallen Tears."

1. Works on the yin and yang and five elements theories of cosmology and divination, so called because they were said to have been recovered from the Yellow and Lo rivers respectively.

16

仲容青雲
CHUNG-JUNG – blue clouds

叔夜玉山
SHU-YEH – a jade mountain

According to the *History of the Chin*, Juan Hsien, whose polite name was Chung-jung, was a native of Wei-shih in Ch'en-liu.

Relaxed and broadminded, he did not bother about petty restraints, and joined his uncle Juan Chi in the outings in the bamboo grove.[1] The people of the time spoke disapprovingly of his conduct. Juan Hsien and his uncle Juan Chi lived on the south side of the road, while another branch of the Juan family lived on the north side. The Juans to the north were rich, those to the south poor. On the seventh day of the seventh month the Juans to the north hung out all their clothes to air, as was the custom, and the brocades and fine silks were enough to dazzle the eye. "One must go along with custom!" said Juan Hsien, and proceeded to hang out his loincloth of coarse hemp on a pole in the courtyard.

Eventually Juan Hsien advanced to the post of assistant to the gentlemen in constant attendance and supplementary cavalrymen. He had an extraordinary understanding of music and was skilled at playing the *p'i-pa* or balloon-guitar. Though he lived in ordinary society, he did not mingle with others. Only with his truly close friends would he gather to play musical instruments, sing, drink, and feast.

The high official Hsün Hsü would often discuss matters pertaining to the musical scales with Juan Hsien, but he came to realize that he was no match for the latter. Much annoyed, he had Juan Hsien dispatched from the capital and assigned to the post of governor of Chih-p'ing. Among Yen Yen-nien's "Songs of the Five Gentlemen," that dealing with Juan Hsien reads:

> *Chung-jung – a blue cloud capacity,[2]*
> *one of those truly born with greatness.*
> *How deep his understanding of music –*
> *he grasped the subtleties of performance!*
> *Kuo Yi was drunk at heart with admiration,*

51

Lord Shan did not fail to eye him closely.
Often recommended, he held no office,
but one wave from Hsün Hsü and off he went to be governor.

Hsi K'ang of the Chin, whose polite name was Shu-yeh, was a man of unusual talent who far surpassed the common crowd. He had a beautiful manner of speaking and a refined bearing, but his dress and appearance were wholly plain and without any attempt at adornment. People regarded him as a dragon or a phoenix, one whose qualities were natural and bestowed by Heaven. Of quiet disposition and few desires, he bore with insult and took no notice of faultfinders, a man of tolerance and great capacity. He was widely read and of copious knowledge, and in his adult years developed a particular fondness for the teachings of Lao Tzu and Chuang Tzu. He was related by marriage to the ruling house of the state of Wei and was appointed to the office of Chung-san counselor. His only close friends were Juan Chi and Shan T'ao, and through them he became a member of the group that included Hsiang Hsiu, Liu Ling, Juan Hsien, and Wang Jung and took part in outings in the bamboo grove. The people of the time referred to them as the Seven Worthies of the Bamboo Grove.

Wang Jung lived for twenty years at Shan-yang, where Hsi K'ang also lived, and during that time he never once saw Hsi K'ang display any sign of either joy or anger. The *Shih-shuo hsin-yü* or *New Specimens of Contemporary Talk* records that Hsi K'ang as a man was lofty and stern, like a solitary pine standing alone. In his drunkenness he would sway magnificently, like a mountain of jade about to crash down.[3]

1. The spot where a semi-legendary group of poet-scholars known as the Seven Worthies of the Bamboo Grove would gather to drink, make music, and discuss philosophy; see the following episode.
2. The capacity to rise to great heights. The "Songs of the Five Gentlemen" by Yen Yen-nien or Yen Yen-chih (A.D. 384–456) deal with five of the Seven Worthies of the Bamboo Grove and are preserved in *Wen hsüan* 21.
3. The *Jung-chih* chapter of the *Shih-shuo hsin-yü*, where the description is attributed to Shan T'ao. Hsi K'ang lived from 223 to 262.

17

江革巨孝

CHIANG KO – immensely filial

王覽友弟

WANG LAN – kind and brotherly

Chiang Ko of the Later Han, whose polite name was Tz'u-weng, was a native of Lin-tzu in the old state of Ch'i.

His father died when he was young, leaving him and his mother alone in the world. When the time of troubles came, he put his mother on his back and fled in search of safety, pushing his way through the most rugged and remote areas, gleaning and gathering whatever he could in the way of food. Several times they encountered bandits who threatened to take Chiang Ko off with them, but each time he would weep and beg to be excused because of his aged mother. His words were so earnest and sincere that they never failed to move his listeners, and the bandits could not bring themselves to use force. Eventually he made his way to Hsia-p'i where, reduced to utter poverty, he worked shoeless and half-naked as a hired laborer in order to provide for his mother.

Toward the end of the *chien-wu* era [A.D. 25–55], he returned with his mother to his native village. Each year at the appropriate season he and his mother had to appear before the district officials for census inspection. Because of his mother's age, Chiang Ko did not wish to see her jolted about in the cart and so he would never use a horse or ox, but would take up the shafts himself and pull the cart to town. As a result of this he came to be known in the area as "Chiang, the immensely filial."

After his mother's death, he was chosen as a man of "worth and goodness, honesty and uprightness," and in time became a chief clerk to the minister of works. Emperor Chang [A.D. 76–88] admired him and treated him with great respect, appointing him to the post of admonisher and granting him special permission to return home at intervals to rest. Chiang Ko, however, declined the appointment on grounds of illness. Each year in the eighth month one of the chief clerks would be sent to his home to inquire of his health and to present him with gifts of lamb and wine. Thus he lived out his days, his reputation for "immensely filial" conduct known throughout the empire.

Wang Lan of the Chin, whose polite name was Hsüan-t'ung, had an elder half-brother named Wang Hsiang whom his mother, a woman of the Chu family, treated with great harshness. When he was still no more than a few years old, Lan would see his brother Hsiang being whipped with thorns. At such times he would cling to his brother and weep, admonishing his mother, and as a result she became a little less cruel and violent in her treatment. Frequently his mother would assign impossible tasks to his brother, whereupon Lan would join in and share the work. In later years the mother would also work Hsiang's wife mercilessly, but at such times Lan's wife would come forward and help her sister-in-law with the work. The mother, frustrated in her designs, would then desist.

After the death of the father, Hsiang began gradually to gain a reputation in the world, and the mother came to hate him even more. She attempted to do away with him in secret by poisoning his wine, but Lan, knowing what she was up to, immediately rose from his place and snatched the wine from his brother. Hsiang, suspecting that the wine was poisoned, struggled to retrieve it from his brother, but the latter would not give it up. The mother thereupon hastily grabbed the wine cup and dumped it over. After this, whenever the mother would serve any food to Hsiang, Lan would always make certain to taste it first.

Lan had a reputation for filial piety, brotherliness, courtesy, and circumspection second only to that of his brother Hsiang. He entered official life and advanced to the post of counselor to the keeper of the palace gate. On retirement, he was granted the privilege of using *chevaux-de-frise* to protect the gate of his house.

18

葛豐刺舉
Chu-ko Feng presses the investigation

息躬歷詆
Hsi-fu Kung criticizes each in turn

Chu-ko Feng of the Former Han, whose polite name was Shao-chi, was a native of Lang-ya.

Having passed the examination as an "expert in the Classics," he was appointed a man of learning of his province. Emperor Yüan [48–33 B.C.] selected him to serve as subordinate commander in charge of convicts. He would press the investigation of criminal charges with great severity regardless of who might be involved. As a result, people in the capital used to say to one another, "Quite some time since I've met you! Did that Chu-ko fellow get you?"

The emperor admired Chu-ko Feng's integrity and granted him the additional post and stipend of counselor to the keeper of the palace gate.

Hsi-fu Kung of the Former Han, whose polite name was Tzu-wei, was a native of Ho-yang in Ho-nei.

In his youth he became a disciple of the erudites and received instruction in the *Spring and Autumn Annals*. In addition, he was widely read in other works of history and philosophy. Emperor Ai [6 B.C.–A.D. 1] selected him to serve as subordinate commander in charge of convicts and steward of the palace. He submitted a memorial to the emperor in which he criticized each of the lords and high officials of the government one by one. It read: "As things stand at present, the chancellor Wang Chia, robust enough in health, is pusillanimous and niggardly in his handling of affairs and quite unfit for his job. The imperial secretary Chia Yen is indolent, weak-kneed, and incapable of carrying out his duties. The general of the left Kung-sun Lu and the commander of convicts Pao Hsüan both have an outward reputation for being forthright and decisive, but in fact are totally ignorant in affairs of state. As for the lesser officials under these men, they are too stupid and mediocre to be worth discussing. If some enemy armed with strong crossbows should suddenly surround the capital and level their long halberds at the palace gates, I do not know who Your Majesty could turn to for protection!"

19

管寧割席

KUAN NING cuts the mat in half

和嶠專車

HO CH'IAO hogs the carriage

According to the *Shih-shuo hsin-yü* or *New Specimens of Contemporary Talk*, Kuan Ning, whose polite name was Yu-an, was helping his friend Hua Hsin to hoe a plot of land and plant a vegetable garden when the two of them came upon some pieces of gold in the ground. Kuan Ning went on hoeing away as though they were no different from the ordinary pebbles and bits of tile, but Hua Hsin picked up the pieces and tossed them aside.

Another time the two men were sitting side by side on the same mat reading when someone riding in a fancy carriage and wearing the cap of a high official passed the gate. Kuan Ning went on reading as before, but Hua Hsin laid aside his book and looked after the carriage. Kuan Ning thereupon cut the mat in half and made two separate seats out of it, saying, "You're no friend of mine!"

Kuan Ning, Hua Hsin, and Ping Yüan all traveled abroad for the purpose of study and the three were very close to one another. The people of the time consequently spoke of them as "a single dragon," explaining that Kuan Ning was the dragon's head, Ping Yüan the dragon's belly, and Hua Hsin the dragon's tail.[1]

Ho Ch'iao of the Chin, whose polite name was Ch'ang-yü, was a native of Hsi-p'ing in Ju-nan.

In his youth he was very distinguished and imposing in appearance and took care to conduct himself with dignity and circumspection. Before long he had won wide acclaim in the world, and people both at court and in private circles agreed that he would be a suitable person to rectify the customs of the age and reform public morals. Yü Kai, after meeting him, said with a sigh of admiration, "Ch'iao is like a lofty thousand-foot pine. Though its trunk may be full of knots and hollows, if one is building a great mansion, such a tree will serve for the ridgepole and rafters!"

Ho Ch'iao was gradually promoted in office until he became

chief of palace writers. Emperor Wu [A.D. 265–89] deeply respected his abilities and treated him accordingly. From past times it had been the custom for the chief of palace writers and the superintendent of palace writers to ride to court in the same carriage. The superintendent of palace writers at this time was Hsün Hsü, but Ho Ch'iao regarded him as a man of little worth and treated him with contempt. Whenever the two were supposed to ride together, Ho Ch'iao would assume a haughty manner and manage to hog the whole carriage. As a result, from Ho Ch'iao's time on it became the custom for the superintendent and the chief of palace writers to ride in separate carriages.

1. The men were students in the reign of Emperor Ling (A.D. 168–88) of the Later Han.

20

時 苗 留 犢
Shih Miao leaves behind a calf

羊 續 懸 魚
Yang Hsü hangs up a fish

According to the *Wei lüeh* or *Summary of Wei*, Shih Miao, whose polite name was Te-chou, was a native of Chü-lu. As a youth he was pure and upright in conduct and had an innate hatred of evil.

During the *chien-an* era [A.D. 196–220], he became magistrate of Shou-ch'un, and the whole district bowed before his virtuous influence like grass before a wind. When he first arrived in the district to take up his post, he was riding in a shabby wicker-top cart drawn by a yellow cow and loaded with a hemp duffel bag of personal belongings. A year or so later, the cow bore a calf. When Shih Miao concluded his term of office, he left the calf behind, explaining to his secretary, "I had no calf when I came as magistrate. The calf was born here and belongs to the district!" The people of the time all thought he was overdoing it, but as a result his name became known throughout the empire. Later he advanced to the post of general of palace attendants.

Yang Hsü of the Later Han, whose polite name was Hsing-tsu, was a native of P'ing-yang in T'ai-shan and became governor of Nan-yang.

In issuing government orders and directives, he was careful to consider the welfare and profit of the people of the province, and as a result the common people admired and obeyed him. He always wore shabby clothing, ate simple food, and went about in a dilapidated carriage drawn by a lean horse. One of the clerks in the provincial office once presented him with a fresh fish. Yang Hsü accepted the gift and then hung it up in the courtyard. Later, when the clerk came again with a similar gift, Yang Hsü showed him the earlier fish that had been hanging in the courtyard, thus putting a stop to any ideas the clerk might have.

Emperor Ling [A.D. 168–88] wanted to appoint him to the post of grand commandant. At this time anyone appointed to one of the three highest posts in the government, which included that of grand commandant, was expected to send a present of ten million cash to the Eastern Garden.[1] A special messenger from the palace known as the Tso-tsou or "Knight of the Left" would be dispatched to make certain that the money was ready. When he arrived at someone's house he would always be treated with great respect and courtesy and presented with generous gifts and bribes. When the messenger arrived at Yang Hsü's house, however, Hsü seated him on a single mat, waved an old quilted robe at him, and said, "This is all the goods you'll get from me!" For this reason, Yang Hsü was never promoted to a high ministerial post.

1. An office had been set up in the Eastern Garden of the palace where, under the guise of "gifts," money was collected in exchange for appointment to various public offices. The practice, begun under Emperor Ling's predecessor, Emperor Huan (A.D. 147–67), was necessitated, it is said, by the fiscal plight of the government.

21

樊噲排闥

FAN K'UAI knocks down the door

辛毗引裾

HSIN P'I pulls at the hem

Fan K'uai of the Former Han was a native of P'ei.

Originally he had made his living as a dog butcher,[1] but later he assisted Emperor Kao-tsu, the founder of the Han, in seizing control of the empire, and was rewarded by being enfeoffed as marquis of Wu-yang. Once Emperor Kao-tsu fell ill and, troubled at the thought of having to see people, took to his bed within the inner palace, giving orders to the doormen not to admit any of the officials. As a result, Chou P'o, Kuan Ying, and the other important ministers for a period of ten days or more were unable to get in to see him. Finally Fan K'uai knocked down the door and marched straight into the bedchamber, the high officials following after him. The emperor was lying alone, his head resting on the lap of a eunuch.

Fan K'uai and the others, tears streaming down their faces, said, "Long ago when Your Majesty and the rest of us rose up from Feng and P'ei and struggled to seize the empire, how brave you were! But now that the empire is already yours, how weary and dispirited you've grown! Moreover, now when you are so ill, you do not meet with us and the other officials to plan for the future, but instead apparently intend to pass away with only this one eunuch by your side. Have you perhaps not heard of the Chao Kao affair?"[2] The emperor laughed and rose from the bed.

Earlier, when Kao-tsu had already seized control of the area within the Han-ku Pass, his rival Hsiang Yü, arriving in the vicinity, was furious and planned to attack him. Kao-tsu, accompanied by a hundred or so horsemen, went to Hung-men to meet with Hsiang Yü. Hsiang Yü's advisor Fan Tseng ordered Hsiang Chuang to draw his sword and perform a sword dance, hoping he could find an opportunity to strike at Kao-tsu. But Hsiang Po rose and danced at the same time, constantly shielding and protecting Kao-tsu with his own body.

Fan K'uai, hearing that the situation was tense, grasped his

61

shield and pushed his way into the gathering, highly enraged. Hsiang Yü, admiring his bravery, presented him with a large goblet of wine and a piece of pork shoulder. Fan K'uai drank the wine, pulled out his sword, and began to cut up the pork and eat it. Asked if he would like more wine, he replied, "I would not hesitate if you offered me death! Why should I refuse a mere cup of wine?" When Kao-tsu went to the privy, he motioned to Fan K'uai to leave at the same time. Kao-tsu mounted a horse, and Fan K'uai and the others accompanied him on foot, hastening along the edge of Mount Li until they returned to Kao-tsu's camp at Pa-shang. If it had not been for Fan K'uai that day, Kao-tsu might have found himself in serious trouble.[3]

According to the *Account of Wei*, Hsin P'i, whose polite name was Tso-chih, was a native of Yang-ti in Ying-ch'uan.

When Emperor Wen of the Wei came to the throne [A.D. 220], Hsin P'i was appointed an attendant in the inner palace. The emperor at this time wished to move some 100,000 gentry families from the Chi-chou region of the north and settle them in Ho-nan in order to repopulate that area. But there had been plagues of locusts for several years in a row, the people were starving, and the officials insisted that the time was not right for such a step. The emperor, however, was quite determined to go ahead with it. When Hsin P'i and the other court officials went in a group and requested an audience, the emperor knew that they had come to reprimand him. He therefore received them with a very irate expression, and none of them dared to speak up. Only Hsin P'i said, "Your Majesty, not considering me to be completely worthless, has placed me among your attendants and assigned me to a post by your side where I may offer my opinion and counsel. Why, then, do you never consult my opinion? I do not speak out of private considerations but only with the welfare of the altars of the soil and grain in mind!"

The emperor made no reply, but rose from his seat and turned to withdraw to his inner apartments. Hsin P'i, however, followed after him, pulling at the hem of his robe. Finally, the emperor jerked the robe out of Hsin P'i's grasp and, without turning around, left the room. After a long time, he reappeared and said to Hsin P'i, "Why are you so adamant in opposing me?"

"If you move the families now," Hsin P'i replied, "you will lose the hearts of the people, and then they will cease to support you."[4] In the end the emperor moved only half the number originally planned.

Once Hsin P'i was attending the emperor when he was out shooting pheasants. The emperor exclaimed, "Shooting pheasants is so delightful!"

"Very delightful for Your Majesty, very troublesome for the officials!" said Hsin P'i. The emperor was silent, but after that he seldom went out pheasant shooting any more.

At the time of his death Hsin P'i held the post of colonel of the guard.

1. Dogs were raised to be eaten.
2. In 210 B.C. when the First Emperor of the Ch'in died while on a tour, the powerful eunuch Chao Kao, acting in collusion with the prime minister, managed to conceal the fact of his death and issue counterfeit edicts in his name, changing his choice for heir and working other mischief.
3. The dramatic meeting between Hsiang Yü and his rival, the future Emperor Kao-tsu of the Han, is one of the most celebrated episodes in early Chinese history, and Han tomb murals have recently been excavated that appear to be representations of the scene. The description has been expanded slightly in the light of parallel passages that give a fuller account, such as that translated in my *Records of the Historian: Chapters from the Shih chi of Ssu-ma Ch'ien* (New York: Columbia University Press 1969), pp. 82–86.
4. Cf. *Mencius* III A, 4: "Those who labor with their minds govern others; those who labor with their strength are governed by others. Those who are governed by others support them; those who govern others are supported by them."

22

孫 楚 漱 石

SUN CH'U rinses his mouth with a stone

郝 隆 曬 書

HO LUNG suns his books

According to the *History of the Chin*, Sun Ch'u, whose polite name was Tzu-ching, was a native of Chung-tu in T'ai-yüan.

He had extraordinary literary ability and a vigorous and high-minded disposition far removed from that of ordinary men. But because he tended at times to be rather overbearing, he failed to win much praise from the people of his community. He was forty when he first joined the staff of the Chen-tung general, and died in the post of governor of Fu-feng.

Earlier, when he was still a young man, he wanted to retire and live the life of a recluse. He intended to tell his friend Wang Chi that he was going to "pillow his head on a stone and rinse his mouth in the stream." But he got mixed up and instead announced that he was going to "rinse his mouth with a stone and pillow his head on a stream." When Wang Chi objected that streams are not for pillowing one's head or rocks for rinsing one's mouth, Sun Ch'u replied, "By pillowing my head on a stream I can wash my ears, and by rinsing my mouth with a stone I can polish my teeth!"[1]

According to the *Shih-shuo hsin-yü* or *New Specimens of Contemporary Talk*, on the seventh day of the seventh month, when people customarily aired household belongings, Ho Lung would go out and lie down on his back in the sun. When people asked him what he was doing, he replied, "I'm sunning the books in my belly!"[2]

1. The washing of the ears refers to an old legend of the sage recluse Hsü Yu who, when asked by Emperor Yao to take over the throne, hastily went and washed out his ears to cleanse them of such a vile suggestion. The Japanese novelist Natsume Sōseki (1867–1916) took his literary name Sōseki, which means "rinse with a stone," from this episode, evidently because he admired Sun Ch'u and the recluse ideal.
2. The Chinese speak of a learned man as having a "bellyful of books."

23

袁盎卻坐
Yüan Ang pulls back the seat

衞瓘撫牀
Wei Kuan pats the couch

Yüan Ang of the Former Han, whose polite name was Ssu, was a native of An-ling.

During the reign of Emperor Wen [179–157 B.C.] he became a general of palace attendants. The emperor was one time paying a visit to the Shang-lin Park, accompanied by the empress and his favorite concubine Lady Shen. In the inner rooms of the palace it was customary for the empress and Lady Shen to sit with their mats side by side as though they were equals. After the mats had been laid out in the officials' lodge in the park, however, Yüan Ang pulled Lady Shen's mat back a little way from that of the empress. Lady Shen was furious and refused to take her seat, and the emperor also rose from his seat in anger. Yüan Ang, anxious to explain his action, came forward and said, "I have heard that only when the proper hierarchical distinctions are observed is there harmony between superiors and inferiors. Now Your Majesty has already chosen an empress, while Lady Shen is no more than a concubine. How is it possible that a concubine and her mistress should sit side by side? Your Majesty is pleased with Lady Shen and naturally you wish to shower her with favors. But though you believe you are doing it for her sake, you may in fact be bringing disaster upon her. Has Your Majesty alone not seen the 'human pig'?"[1]

The emperor was pleased and went and explained what Yüan Ang had said to Lady Shen. She in turn rewarded Yüan Ang with a gift of fifty catties of gold. But Yüan Ang continued time and again to admonish the emperor in this fashion, and as a result he was not permitted to stay for long at court.

According to the *History of the Chin*, Wei Kuan, whose polite name was Po-yü, was a native of An-i in Ho-tung.

In the time of Emperor Wu [A.D. 265–89] he was advanced to the post of minister of works. His conduct of official business was marked by strict honesty and directness, and he was highly praised in both court and private circles. At this time the future Emperor Hui was still heir apparent. The court officials all regarded him as a dull-witted young man who should never be allowed to handle affairs of government. Wei Kuan had for some time wanted to propose to the emperor that the young man be removed from the position of heir apparent, but he did not have the courage to speak out. Some time later, a banquet was held at the Terrace Overtopping the Clouds. Wei Kuan, pretending to be drunk, took the opportunity to kneel before the couch upon which the emperor was seated, saying, "There's something I wish to propose!" Three times he tried to speak, but each time he stopped. Finally he patted the couch with his hand and said, "This seat should not go to just anyone!"

The emperor perceived his meaning, but deliberately pretended not to understand, saying, "You really are very drunk, aren't you!" Wei Kuan said nothing further.

Empress Chia, the heir apparent's mother, as a result of this came to hate Wei Kuan. Later Wei Kuan applied for permission to retire from official life on grounds of old age. He was advanced to the rank of grand guardian and retired to his home. When Emperor Hui came to the throne, he put Wei Kuan in charge of the office of palace writers. But Emperor Hui's mother Empress Chia had from times past borne Wei Kuan a grudge, and moreover she feared that, because of his integrity and outspokenness, she would not be able to continue to indulge her cruel and lascivious ways. She therefore spoke to the emperor and had him issue an edict relieving Wei Kuan of his official duties. Eventually Wei Kuan was put to death.

1. A reference to Lady Ch'i, the favorite concubine of Emperor Wen's father Emperor Kao-tsu. After Kao-tsu's death, she was horribly mutilated by his consort Empress Lü, thrown into a pigsty, and titled the "human pig."

24

于公高門
LORD YÜ raises the gate

曹參趣裝
Ts'AO Ts'AN hurries to pack

Yü Ting-kuo of the Former Han, whose polite name was Man-ch'ien, was a native of T'an in Tung-hai.

His father Lord Yü had been district prison official and a judge of criminal cases for the province and was very fair in his administration of justice. Whenever a case was brought before the officials, if Lord Yü handed down the decision, none of the parties had cause for resentment. While he was still living a shrine was erected to him in the province.[1]

Earlier, the gate to the neighborhood where Lord Yü and his family lived fell into disrepair. When the elders of the community gathered together to rebuild it, Lord Yü said, "Make it a little bigger and taller, with room enough to admit a team of four horses and a high topped carriage. In deciding criminal cases I have done many unknown kindnesses and I've never inflicted injustice upon anyone. My sons and grandson are bound to come up in the world!" As it turned out, his son Yü Ting-kuo became chancellor in the time of Emperor Hsüan [73–49 B.C.] and was enfeoffed as marquis of Hsi-p'ing. Yü Ting-kuo's son Yü Yung became imperial secretary, and the marquisate passed down in the family from generation to generation.

Ts'ao Ts'an of the Former Han was a native of P'ei. He served under Emperor Kao-tsu and in reward for his accomplishments he received the split tallies enfeoffing him as marquis of P'ing-yang. When Kao-tsu's eldest son Liu Fei was made king of Ch'i, Ts'ao Ts'an served as his prime minister. During the nine years he held this office, the state of Ch'i enjoyed peace and stability and he won wide acclaim as a worthy minister. Later, Hsiao Ho, the prime minister of the Han court, died [193 B.C.]. When Ts'ao Ts'an received the news he told his servants, "Hurry and make ready for the journey, for I will soon be going to the capital to become the new prime minister!" Shortly after, as Ts'ao Ts'an had predicted, a summons came from the court appointing him the new prime minister to replace Hsiao Ho. He made no changes whatsoever in the management of affairs, conducting everything exactly in accordance with the rules that Hsiao Ho had laid down.

When Ts'ao Ts'an died, the common people composed a song that went:

> *Hsiao Ho made us laws,*
> *plain as the figure "one;"*
> *Ts'ao Ts'an took his place,*
> *saw that they weren't undone,*
> *governed in purity and stillness,*
> *brought peace to us everyone!*

1. After eminent and worthy men died, shrines were often erected to them in the places where they had lived or worked, but this is said to be the earliest case in which a shrine was erected to a man while he was still alive.

25

庶女振風
A common maid stirs up the wind

鄒衍降霜
Tsou Yen makes the frost fall

The *Huai-nan Tzu* says: A common maid appealed to Heaven and thunder and lightning came striking down. Duke Ching of Ch'i fell from his terrace, breaking and injuring his arms and legs, and the waters of the sea overflowed in abundance.

Hsü Shen comments on this passage as follows: She was an ordinary woman of humble station, a widow of the state of Ch'i. She had no children but declined to remarry, instead waiting on her mother-in-law with great diligence and respect. Her mother-in-law had no surviving sons, but she had a daughter who hoped to inherit her property. The daughter therefore did her best to make the widow remarry, but the latter adamantly refused. The daughter then murdered her mother and laid the blame on the widow. The widow was unable to prove her innocence and, overcome with feelings of injustice, she appealed to Heaven.

Tsou Yen served King Hui of the state of Yen, but the king's associates slandered him. He was bound and thrown into prison, where he turned his eyes toward Heaven and wept. Although it was the height of summer, Heaven in response caused a frost to fall.

Chiang Yen says in his letter, "Long ago a humble minister beat his breast, and flying frost fell over the land of Yen; a common maid appealed to Heaven, and a stirring wind struck the hall of Ch'i."[1]

1. From a letter by Chiang Yen (A.D. 444–505) addressed to the king of Chien-p'ing and preserved in *Wen hsüan* 39.

69

26

詰汾興魏
CHIEH-FEN founds the Wei
鼈令王蜀
PIEH LING becomes king of Shu

According to the *Pei shih* or *Northern History*, Emperor Sheng-wu of the Wei bore the personal name Chieh-fen.[1]

He was once out hunting among the hills and lakes when he spied a curtained carriage coming down from the sky. When it reached the ground, a beautiful lady appeared from it. She said she was a daughter of Heaven who had been ordered to mate with him. At dawn of the following day she asked for permission to return to her home, promising to meet with Chieh-fen at the same spot when a year had passed. Having finished speaking, she departed. When the time for the meeting arrived, Chieh-fen proceeded to the place where he had previously hunted. The daughter of Heaven appeared according to her promise and presented him with a child which she had borne, saying, "This is your son. He and his heirs shall be rulers for generations to come!" With these words she took her leave.

The son became Emperor Shen-yüan, also known as the First Ancestor. For this reason there was a saying among the people of the time, "Emperor Chieh-fen had no in-laws, Emperor Li-wei had no maternal uncles." Li-wei was the personal name of Emperor Shen-yüan.

According to the *Basic Annals of the King of Shu*, there was a man of the Ching region named Pieh Ling who died. His corpse disappeared into the waters of the Yangtze and, following the river upstream until it reached Ch'eng-tu, came to life again and appeared before Tu Yü, the king of Shu. The king made him his prime minister. Tu Yü, who titled himself Emperor Wang, realized that he was no match for Pieh Ling in virtue and accordingly ceded the throne of Shu to him.[2] Pieh Ling titled himself Emperor K'ai-ming, and his descendants for five generations continued to use the title of emperor, but K'ai-ming Shang renounced the title and returned to the earlier appellation of king.

1. A legendary ancestor of the T'o-pa family, which in A.D. 386 founded a dynasty in northern China known as the Northern Wei. The T'o-pa were a branch of the Hsien-pi, who were probably proto-Mongol people. The titles borne by Chieh-fen and his son were given to them many years later by their descendants and do not mean that they ever actually reigned as emperors.

2. According to another version of this legend, Emperor Wang ordered Pieh Ling to bring the flood waters under control, and in the meantime debauched Pieh Ling's wife. Ashamed of his deeds, he abdicated his throne to Pieh Ling. When he took his leave, the bird called a *chüan*, variously translated as nightjar or cuckoo, was crying, and the people of Shu hence associate its sad cry with the fate of Emperor Wang. Some say that when Emperor Wang died his soul turned into a cuckoo, which has given rise to many suggestive names for the bird such as "soul of Shu" or *pu-ju-kuei* ("Better go home!"), the latter imitative of its cry. In Japan these names are applied to the bird known as the *hototogisu*.

27

不疑誣金

Pu-i is accused of stealing money

卞和泣玉

Pien Ho weeps over the jade

Chih Pu-i of the Former Han was a native of Nan-yang. He became a palace attendant in the service of Emperor Wen [179–157 B.C.]. Once one of the officials who lived in the same dormitory with Chih Pu-i was going home on vacation and mistakenly picked up someone else's money and went off with it. When the owner of the money discovered his loss he accused Chih Pu-i, who confessed to the theft and, apologizing, procured the sum and reimbursed the owner. Later, when the official came back from his vacation and returned the original money, the owner was deeply chagrined at his mistake and Chih Pu-i received wide praise for his worthy action. He was gradually advanced until he reached the position of palace counselor.

One time when the officials were gathered in court someone tried to slander Chih Pu-i by saying, "He is certainly good looking, but what can you do with a man who carries on in secret with his older brother's wife?"

When Chih Pu-i heard of the remark he said, "As a matter of fact, I have no older brother," but he was unwilling to go to any further trouble to clear himself of the charge. In the latter part of Emperor Wen's reign he became imperial secretary.

According to the *Han Fei Tzu*, there was once a man of Ch'u named Mr. Ho who, having found a piece of jade matrix in the Ch'u Mountains, took it to court and presented it to King Li.[1] King Li instructed the jeweler to examine it, and the jeweler reported, "It's only a stone!" The king, supposing that Ho was trying to deceive him, ordered that his left foot be cut off in punishment.

Later, when King Wu came to the throne of Ch'u, Ho once more took his matrix and presented it to King Wu. King Wu ordered his jeweler to examine it, and again the jeweler reported, "It's only a stone!" The king, supposing that Ho was again trying

72

to practice deception, ordered that his right foot be cut off.

When King Wen came to the throne, Ho, clasping the matrix to his breast, went to the foot of the Ch'u Mountains, where he wept for three days and nights, and when all his tears were cried out, he wept blood in their place. The king, hearing of this, sent someone to question him. "Many people in the world have had their feet amputated. Why do you weep so piteously over it?" the man asked.

Ho replied, "I do not grieve because my feet have been cut off. I grieve because a precious jewel is dubbed a mere stone, and a man of integrity is called a deceiver. This is why I weep!" The king then ordered the jeweler to cut and polish the matrix, and when he had done so a precious jewel emerged. Eventually it came to be known as "The Jade of Mr. Ho."

1. Mr. Ho's name is given as Pien Ho in other versions of this famous anecdote.

28

檀卿沐猴

T'AN CH'ING makes like a monkey

謝尚鴝鵒

HSIEH SHANG does the mynah bird

When Hsü Po of the Former Han, who had been granted the title of marquis of P'ing-en, moved into his new mansion, the chancellor, the imperial secretary, the generals, and the high officials of the two-thousand-picul class all went to congratulate him.[1] Only Kai K'uan-jao, the subordinate commander in charge of convicts, failed to appear. Hsü Po had to urge him specifically to come before he would do so. He entered from the west stairway and took the seat of honor facing east. Hsü Po in person poured wine for him, saying, "Lord Kai has to catch up with the rest of us."

"Don't pour me a big drink!" said Kai K'uan-jao. "I might go mad with the effects of the wine!"

The chancellor Wei Hsiang laughed and said, "You're mad enough sober – no need for any wine!" All the guests turned disparaging eyes toward Kai K'uan-jao.

When the drinking and merriment had reached its height, T'an Chang-ch'ing, the privy treasurer of the Palace of Lasting Trust, rose and performed a dance which represented a monkey fighting with a dog. All the guests roared with laughter, but Kai K'uan-jao was not amused. Instead he rose, hurried from the gathering, and submitted a memorial to the throne accusing T'an of performing a monkey dance while occupying a high official position, an act of the greatest rudeness and disrespect. Emperor Hsüan [73–49 B.C.] wanted to punish T'an, and it was only after Hsü Po had apologized on his behalf that he was finally excused.

Hsieh Shang of the Chin dynasty, whose polite name was Jen-tsu, had by the age of eight attained the intelligence and understanding of an adult. His father Hsieh K'un once took him along to a farewell party for some friends. One of the guests remarked, "This boy is the Yen Hui of the whole gathering today!"[2] But Hsieh Shang said, "Since there is no Master Confucius present, how can one tell who is a Yen Hui?" The guests were startled and impressed.

When Hsieh Shang grew up, he was very good at music and had a broad command of the various arts. Wang Tao compared him to Wang Jung, one of the Seven Worthies of the Bamboo Grove, who had held the title of marquis of An-feng, and thus he later came to be referred to as "Little An-feng." Wang Tao selected him to be a clerk in the government office which he headed. When Hsieh Shang first arrived at the office and asked to be allowed to pay his respects to his superior, Wang Tao was at the moment entertaining a group of guests at a banquet. He said to Hsieh Shang, "I've heard that you can do a mynah bird dance. All the guests would very much like to see it." Hsieh Shang thereupon put on a robe, tied his head in a kerchief, and began to dance. Wang Tao instructed the guests to clap their hands and keep time, and Hsieh Shang moved about among them, now looking up, now looking down, intent on his imitation of the mynah bird and quite unmindful of the company. Such was the openness and self-confidence he possessed.

At the time of his death [A.D. 357] he had advanced to the post of general of the guard and gentleman in constant attendance and supplementary cavalryman.

1. Hsü Po was the maternal grandfather of the heir apparent, later Emperor Yüan. I have expanded the account from Kai K'uan-jao's biography in *Han shu* 77 and omitted the latter part. Kai's surname may also be read Ko.
2. Yen Hui was among the youngest and most brilliant of Confucius's disciples.

29 WANG SHUN's embroidered quilt

張氏銅鉤

MR. CHANG's copper sash hook

Wang Shun of the Later Han, whose polite name was Shao-lin, was a native of Hsin-tu in Kuang-han.[1]

He was once visiting the capital when he came upon a student in an empty house looking ill and worn. Moved to pity, Wang Shun did what he could to take care of him. "I was on my way to Lo-yang when I fell ill," the student told Wang Shun, "and I may die at any moment. There are ten catties of gold under my belt. I want to give them to you. After I am dead, I beg you to bury my bones!" Before Shun could ask what his family or personal name was, the student died. Shun used one catty of the gold to cover the funeral expenses and placed the remainder of the gold in the coffin. No one knew about the affair.

Later Shun was appointed head of the post station in Ta-tu. When he first arrived at Ta-tu, a horse galloped into the post station and came to a halt. The day was very windy and presently an embroidered quilt whirled through the air and dropped down, coming to rest, like the horse, in front of Wang Shun. Shun handed the horse and quilt over to the district officials along with a report on the matter, but they returned them to Shun. Later Shun mounted the horse and set off for the district of Lo. The horse in time began to race wildly and carried Shun into a completely strange house. When the master of the house saw them, he exclaimed, "Now I've caught the thief!" The man then asked Shun how he had come into possession of the horse, and Shun recounted everything that had happened, explaining also about the embroidered quilt. The master looked rather disgruntled and then, after some time, said, "The quilt blew away in the wind and the horse went off with it. But what secret act of merit have you performed that you should come into possession of these two objects?"

Shun then recalled how he had buried the student. He therefore told the master of that affair as well, describing the student's appearance and explaining where the gold was buried.

The master in great astonishment exclaimed, "That was my son! His family name was Chin and his personal name Yen. Some time ago he went off to the capital but I have never known what became of him. And to think that it was you who buried him! Because this great debt of gratitude has for so long gone unrequited, Heaven took this means to bring your virtue to light." As a result of this, Wang Shun became famous and advanced in service to the position of clerk in charge of documents for the province.

According to the *San-fu chüeh-lu* or *Definitive Record of the Three Districts of Ch'ang-an*, one of the ancestors of the Chang family of Fu-feng once served as clerk in charge of documents for the province. One morning he had gotten up early and gone to his office when a dove flew down from its perch on the rafters and alighted in front of his desk. The clerk said, "Dove, why have you come? If you bring misfortune, then fly back up to the rafters. But if you bring good luck, then fly into the breast of my robe." So saying, he opened the breast of his robe, whereupon the dove flew into it. When he searched for it, all he could find was a copper sash hook, which he fastened to his girdle.

He rose in office to become governor of several provinces in succession, and eventually was numbered among the nine highest ministers in the government. A stranger from the region of Shu who had come to Ch'ang-an heard of the sash hook and, passing bribes in secret to Mr. Chang's maid, persuaded her to sell it to him. Death and misfortune fell upon the family of the man from Shu who, terrified, returned the sash hook to Mr. Chang. Mr. Chang thereupon rose to the position of a two-thousand-picul official. He later lost the sash hook and the Chang family in the end fell into decline.

1. This anecdote has been clumsily abbreviated from the version in *Hou Han shu* 111; I have restored parts of the abbreviated sections in order to make the narrative intelligible.

30

雍 齒 先 候

YUNG CH'IH is first to be made a marquis

Lord Ting of the Former Han was a native of Hsüeh and a younger half brother of Chi Pu by the same mother. He served as a general under Hsiang Yü and once pursued Kao-tsu, Hsiang Yü's rival, west of P'eng-ch'eng. Lord Ting's forces bore down on Kao-tsu and his men and had closed swords with them when Kao-tsu, sorely pressed, turned about and said to Lord Ting, "Why should two worthy men like us harass one another in this way!" Lord Ting accordingly called off his troops and withdrew.

Later, when Hsiang Yü was wiped out, Lord Ting came to visit Kao-tsu. Kao-tsu had him seized and paraded before his army, announcing, "Lord Ting was disloyal in his service to Hsiang Yü. It was he who caused Hsiang Yü to lose the empire!" Then he had Lord Ting beheaded, saying, "I want to make sure that no subject hereafter shall imitate Lord Ting's example!"

Emperor Kao-tsu of the Former Han was once residing at the Southern Palace in Lo-yang when he looked down from a covered walk and saw his generals pacing restlessly back and forth in the courtyard and talking together. He asked his minister Chang Liang what they were doing, whereupon Chang Liang replied, "When Your Majesty rose up from among the common people, it was through these men that you seized control of the empire. Now you have become the Son of Heaven, but those whom you have enfeoffed have all been close friends from old days such as Hsiao Ho and Ts'ao Ts'an, while all those whom you have executed were your lifelong enemies. These followers of yours fear that you will not be willing to enfeoff all of them, or are apprehensive lest they be suspected of some error and be condemned to execution. Therefore they gather together in this way to plot rebellion. Among the men whom you have always disliked, and whom your followers know you dislike, whom do you hate the most?"

The emperor replied, "Yung Ch'ih and I are ancient enemies. Many times in the past he has brought me trouble and shame. I would like to have killed him, but because his merit is great I have not had the heart."

"You must hurry and enfeoff Yung Ch'ih before anyone else, and make what you have done known to your other followers. Then they will feel assured of their own rewards," said Chang Liang.

The emperor thereupon held a feast and enfeoffed Yung Ch'ih as marquis of Shih-fang, at the same time ordering the prime minister and the imperial secretary to settle the question of rewards and carry out the remainder of the enfeoffments with all dispatch. When the other followers of the emperor left the banquet, they said to each other happily, "If even Yung Ch'ih can get to be a marquis, the rest of us have nothing to worry about!"

31

陳 雷 膠 漆
CH'EN and LEI – glue and lacquer

范 張 雞 黍
FAN and CHANG – chicken and millet

Ch'en Chung of the Later Han, whose polite name was Ching-kung, was a native of I-ch'un in Yü-chang. In his youth he became friends with Lei Yi of P'o-yang, whose polite name was Chung-kung.

The governor of the province recommended Ch'en Chung for official service as a man of "filial conduct and integrity." Ch'en Chung wished to decline the honor in favor of Lei Yi, but the governor would not hear of this. The following year Lei Yi was also chosen as a man of "filial conduct and integrity," and both were assigned to the office of gentlemen attendants. Later they were both promoted to the post of gentleman in the office of palace writers. Lei Yi voluntarily accepted the blame for an offense committed by one of his fellow officials and as a result was dismissed from his post. Ch'en Chung, observing his friend's departure, resigned his own post on grounds of illness. Later Lei Yi was once more selected for office as a man of "outstanding talent," but he declined in favor of Ch'en Chung and refused to accept appointment. The people of their hometown used to say of them, "Lacquer and glue bind things together, but make no bond like that between Ch'en and Lei!" Later they were both summoned to the office of the three highest ministers and advanced to the post of clerk to the imperial secretary.

Fan Shih of the Later Han, whose polite name was Chü-ch'ing, was a native of Chin-hsiang in Shan-yang. In his youth he attended the university in the capital and became friends with Chang Shao of Ju-nan, whose polite name was Yüan-po.

Both requested permission to leave the capital and return to their respective homes. Fan Shih said to his friend, "In two years I will be going back to the capital once more, and at that time I will stop to visit you, pay my respects to your parents, and perhaps see a child of your own." The two accordingly fixed a date for the meeting.

Later, when the appointed day drew near, Chang Shao told his mother, "Please prepare the food and wine so that they will be ready when he comes."

But his mother said, "You and your friend have been parted for two years and this promise of yours involves a journey of a thousand miles. How can you be so certain he will keep his word?"

"Chü-ch'ing is a man to be trusted. He would never go back on his promise!" replied Chang Shao.

"In that case," said his mother, "I had better start brewing you some wine."

When the day arrived, Fan Shih appeared just as he had said he would. Shown into the hall, he accepted the wine that was offered to him and enjoyed himself to the full before taking his leave. (The old commentaries mention killing a chicken and cooking millet for the feast, but this is not recorded in the original.)[1]

1. That is, in the biography in *Hou Han shu* 101 from which the anecdote is taken; Hsü Tzu-kuang adds this parenthetical remark in order to explain the phrase "Fan and Chang – chicken and millet" in the *Meng Ch'iu* text.

32

季布一諾
CHI PU's one promise
阮 瞻 三 語
JUAN CHAN's three words

Chi Pu of the Former Han was a native of Ch'u and was famous for his spirited and cavalier behavior. Hsiang Yü put him in charge of a body of troops, and he several times made serious trouble for Hsiang Yü's rival, Emperor Kao-tsu. After Hsiang Yü had been wiped out, Kao-tsu ordered a search made for Chi Pu, offering a reward of a thousand pieces of gold for his capture and threatening that if anyone gave him quarter or hid him, the person would be exterminated along with his three sets of close relatives.[1]

Chi Pu hid at the home of a Mr. Chou of P'u-yang. Mr. Chou shaved Chi Pu's head, put a collar around his neck, dressed him in coarse cloth and, placing him in a covered cart along with twenty or thirty of the slaves from his household, took him to the home of Chu Chia in Lu to sell.

Chu Chia guessed that it was Chi Pu and thereupon went to pay a visit to Lord T'eng, the marquis of Ju-yin. "What crime has Chi Pu committed?" he said to Lord T'eng. "Every subject simply carries out the duties assigned him by his lord. Does the emperor think he can wipe out all of Hsiang Yü's former followers? The emperor has only just won control of the world. If he is to search all over for one man simply because of some private grudge he bears, what an example of pettiness he will be showing!" Lord T'eng reported these words to Kao-tsu. Kao-tsu thereupon pardoned Chi Pu and summoned him to the post of palace attendant. Later Chi Pu was made governor of Ho-tung.

Chi Pu had earlier entertained a considerable distaste for the rhetorician named Master Ts'ao Ch'iu. Ts'ao Ch'iu went to visit him and, bowing only slightly, said, "People in Ch'u have a saying that 'A hundred pieces of pure gold are not as good as one of Chi Pu's promises.' I wonder how you have managed to get such a reputation in this region of Liang and Ch'u? You and I are both men of Ch'u. Now if you had me to spread your reputation abroad in the course of my travels, think what praise you might enjoy! Why do you object to me so?" Chi Pu, very much pleased, invited the man to stay and treated him as his most honored guest.

Juan Chan of the Chin, whose polite name was Ch'ien-li, was the son of Juan Hsien, the governor of Shih-p'ing.

Pure and open in nature, he had few desires and possessed an inner calm and contentment. When reading books he did not try to make a thorough study of them, but silently absorbed their essential points. Called upon to argue a matter of principle, his words appeared inadequate, yet they conveyed a meaning that lingered on after them. He was once given an interview by the minister of education Wang Jung, who said to him, "The sage Confucius in his teachings emphasized the importance of names,[2] while Lao Tzu and Chuang Tzu sought to make clear the state of naturalness. Were their aims identical or were they different?"

Juan Chan replied, "Weren't they identical?"

Wang Jung sighed with admiration for quite some time, and then immediately ordered that Juan Chan be appointed to public office. People of the time accordingly referred to him as the "three-word clerk." During the *yung-chia* era [A.D. 307–12] he became a retainer to the heir apparent.

Juan Chan had always held the theory that spirits do not exist, arguing that only by adopting such a principle could one correctly understand the nature of the seen and the unseen. Suddenly one day a stranger sent in his name and asked for an interview with Juan Chan. Juan Chan engaged the stranger in conversation, and after some time the discussion turned to the matter of ghosts and spirits. Juan Chan refuted the stranger's views with great forcefulness, until the latter was completely at a loss for words. Thereupon he flushed with anger and said, "Ghosts and spirits have been acknowledged by every sage and worthy man of past and present. How can you alone insist they don't exist! As a matter of fact, I myself am a ghost!" With this, he changed into his ghostly form, and after a moment or two faded away into nothing. Juan Chan was filled with horror, and a year or so later he fell ill and died.

1. Though there are varying interpretations of the term "three sets of relatives," it is probable that it refers to the parents, wife and children, and brothers

and sisters of the offender, all of whom would be put to death along with the offender himself.

2. I.e., one's nominal position in society as a ruler or subject, father or son, teacher or student, etc., and the degree to which one lived up to its duties. Juan Chan's three-word affirmation of the essential harmony of Confucian and Taoist teachings is one of the most famous philosophical pronouncements of the period.

33
郭文遊山
KUO WEN strolls the hills
袁宏泊渚
YÜAN HUNG ties up at the beach

According to the *History of the Chin*, Kuo Wen, whose polite name was Wen-chü, was a native of Chih in Ho-nei.

In his youth he loved the mountains and waters and longed for the life of the recluse. Whenever he would go strolling in the hills and forests, he would stay away ten days or more and almost forget to return. After his mother and father died, he declined to marry but instead left home and wandered about visiting famous mountains.

When Lo-yang fell to the northern invaders [A.D. 317], he shouldered his belongings and set off on foot for the south, entering the Ta-pi Mountains in Wu-hsing. He pushed on to the very end of the ravine, where no one lived, and there propped pieces of wood against the trees, rigged a covering of straw mats, and fashioned a home. His shelter had no walls or partitions and was at times invaded by wild beasts, but Kuo Wen continued to live in it all alone for over ten years and in the end suffered no harm. He always dressed in deer skins with a head covering of kudzu vine, drank no wine and ate no meat.

The high official Wang Tao invited him to take up residence in his garden. Kuo Wen complied, but never once ventured out of the garden during his seven years in residence there. Eventually he ran away and made his way back to Lin-an, near his old home in Wu-hsing, and built himself a hut in the mountains.

Yüan Hung of the Chin, whose polite name was Yen-po, was a native of Yang-hsia in Ch'en Province.

He possessed unusual talent and his writings won unqualified praise. The high official Hsieh Shang at this time was exercising control over the region of Ox Beach. One autumn evening, entranced by the moonlight, he and his attendants changed into inconspicuous clothing and went out in a boat on the Yangtze. It happened that Yüan Hung was also out on the river in a catamaran, chanting poetry. Because of the clarity of his voice and the extraordinary beauty of the words, Hsieh Shang sent someone over to inquire who he was and to invite him to join Shang in his boat. The two men, forgetful of sleep, chatted away until day-break. As a result of this incident, Yüan Hung's fame increased daily.

Hsieh Shang's cousin Hsieh An always marveled at the aptness of Yüan Hung's replies and the alacrity he displayed in argu-ment. Later, when Hsieh An was acting as provincial director of Yang-chou, Yüan Hung set off to become governor of Tung-yang Province. Offerings were made to the god of the road and a farewell party was held for him at Chih-t'ing, which was attended by all the worthy men of the time. Hsieh An, curious to observe how Yüan Hung would respond if he were suddenly put on the spot, took hold of his hand in parting and then, turning to his attendants and taking a fan from one of them, he presented it to Yüan Hung, saying, "Just a little gift to take with you."

Yüan Hung replied, "And with it I shall waft a kindly breeze to comfort the humble folk in my care." The people of the time sighed with admiration at the speed and pertinence of the reply.

34

向秀聞笛
Hsiang Hsiu listens to a flute
伯牙絕絃
Po Ya breaks the strings

According to the *History of the Chin*, Hsiang Hsiu, whose polite name was Tzu-ch'i, was a native of Huai in Ho-nei.

Pure and enlightened in nature, he possessed far-reaching understanding. While still a youth, his abilities were recognized by Shan T'ao. He had always been fond of the doctrines of Lao Tzu and Chuang Tzu. But although the "Inner" and "Outer" chapters of the *Chuang Tzu* continued to be perused by generation after generation, no one was capable of discussing the underlying purport of the text. Hsiang Hsiu thereupon prepared explications which revealed the particular excellence of the work and expounded its subtle concepts. Readers of the *Chuang Tzu* were thereafter able to attain a far deeper understanding of the text. Kuo Hsiang made Hsiang Hsiu's interpretations the basis of his own commentary, expanding them at the same time.[1] The doctrines of the Confucians and the Mo-ists came to be looked on with contempt, and the words of the Taoists in the end won the day.

Hsi K'ang was very skillful at forging metal, and Hsiang Hsiu used to act as his assistant, the two of them working away happily as though they were unaware that anyone else existed. After Hsi K'ang was executed [A.D. 262], Hsiang Hsiu visited Lo-yang and wrote a poem in *fu* or rhyme-prose form entitled "Recalling Old Times," in which he said: "Hsi K'ang had a wide mastery of the various arts, and was particularly skilled at string and wind instruments. When he was facing execution, he turned and looked at the shadows cast by the sun, and then called for a lute and played on it. My travels took me to the west, but later I passed by the old houses where he and I used to live. It was the hour when the sun was about to sink into the Springs of Yü, and the cold was harsh and biting. Someone nearby was playing a flute, the sound of it drifting abroad, tenuous and thin. I thought back to the good times we'd had, the banquets and outings of long ago, and, stirred to sadness by the notes of the flute, I decided to write this *fu*."[2]

Later Hsiang Hsiu was made an assistant to the gentlemen in constant attendance and supplementary cavalrymen. Although he resided at court, he did not try to attend to the duties of his office, merely putting in an appearance and letting it go at that.

The *Lieh Tzu* says: Po Ya was good at playing the lute and Chung Tzu-ch'i was good at listening. When Po Ya would play the lute, if his thoughts were on the lofty mountains, Chung Tzu-ch'i would say, "That's it – tall and craggy like Mount T'ai!" If his thoughts were on the flowing waters, Chung Tzu-ch'i would say, "That's it – vast and deep like the Yellow River or the Yangtze!" Whatever Po Ya had in his mind, Chung Tzu-ch'i was certain to guess it.

The *Lü-shih ch'un-ch'iu* or *Spring and Autumn of Mr. Lü* says: When Chung Tzu-ch'i died, Po Ya smashed his lute and broke the strings. For the rest of his life he never again played the lute, because he believed that there was no one worth playing for.

1. Hsiang Hsiu's commentary is no longer extant, though presumably most or all of it was incorporated into the commentary by Kuo Hsiang (d. A.D. 312), the oldest extant commentary on the *Chuang Tzu*.
2. The quotation represents most of the introductory section of the poem; the remainder is in verse. The poem is translated in my *Chinese Rhyme-prose* (New York: Columbia University Press 1971), pp. 61–63.

35

郭 槐 自 屈

Kuo Huai humbles herself

南 康 猶 憐

Nan-k'ang is attracted too

According to the *History of the Chin*, Chia Ch'ung, whose polite name was Kung-lü, was a native of Hsiang-ling in P'ing-yang.

His first wife was the daughter of the high official Li Feng, but when Li Feng was put to death, the other members of the Li family, including Chia Ch'ung's wife, were implicated in the affair as well and were sent into exile. Later, Chia Ch'ung married Kuo Huai, known by the title Lady of Kuang-ch'eng. When Emperor Wu came to the throne to found the Chin dynasty [A.D. 265], the members of the Li family were pardoned and allowed to return from exile. By special order of the emperor, Chia Ch'ung, who now found himself with two wives, prepared to set them up as wife of the left and wife of the right respectively. But Kuo Huai was very jealous by nature and, pushing up her sleeves in anger, she berated her husband, saying, "You have won merit by drawing up the laws and statutes and assisting the emperor to gain the throne, but I had a part in it! What right has that Li woman to be ranked side by side with me?" Chia Ch'ung was thus obliged to build a house for Lady Li in the Yung-p'ing district of the capital and was unable to visit her. When Emperor Wu's son, the future Emperor Hui, was made heir apparent, Chia Ch'ung's daughter by Kuo Huai was chosen to be his consort.

Kuo Huai had always wanted to see what Lady Li looked like, but her husband said, "She is a woman of great talent and bearing. You would do well not to visit her!" After Kuo Huai's daughter had been made consort to the heir apparent, however, Kuo Huai set off in grand style to call on Lady Li. When she entered the door, Lady Li came forward to greet her. Kuo Huai, before she realized what she was doing, assumed a humble posture and ended by performing a double bow before Lady Li. From this time on, whenever her husband went out of the house, Kuo Huai would send someone to keep an eye on him, always fearful that he might go to Lady Li's house. Lady Li was a woman of virtue and

89

beauty who was noted for her ability and exemplary conduct. She wrote a work entitled *Nü hsün* or "Precepts for Women" that was widely read at the time.

According to the *Shih-shuo hsin-yü* or *New Specimens of Contemporary Talk*, Huan Wen married Princess Nan-k'ang, a daughter of Emperor Ming [A.D. 323–25] of the Eastern Chin dynasty. When Huan Wen conquered the region of Shu, he seized the younger sister of Li Shih, who had held power in the region, and made her his concubine. He treated her with great favor and kept her housed in a room behind his detached library. When Princess Nan-k'ang got word of this, she went with several dozen of her maids, a drawn dagger in her hand, intending to make a surprise attack upon her rival. Lady Li was at the moment combing her hair, the long strands hanging down to the floor, and she presented a figure of decorous beauty. When she became aware of the princess, she slowly bound up the strands of hair that had been hanging down to the floor, folded her hands, and turned to the princess, saying, "My native land has been conquered, my family wiped out, and I have been brought here against my will. Should you be kind enough to kill me today, I would welcome it as though it were the gift of life!" Her bearing was calm and poised, her speech filled with a tone of sadness.

The princess thereupon threw down her dagger, stepped forward and embraced her, saying, "Now that I have seen you, even I find you attractive – no wonder that old rascal husband of mine should do so!" After that, she treated Lady Li with kindness.

36

魯恭馴雉

Lu Kung tames the pheasants

宋均去獸

Sung Chün drives off the beasts

Lu Kung of the Later Han, whose polite name was Chung-
k'ang, was a native of P'ing-ling in Fu-feng.

In the time of Emperor Chang [A.D. 76–88] he was appointed
magistrate of the district of Chung-mou. He concentrated on
governing through the influence of virtue and did not rely upon
penalties and punishments. At this time locusts were causing great
damage to the crops in various kingdoms and provinces, zig-
zagging back and forth through one region after another, but they
never entered the district of Chung-mou. When Yüan An, the
governor of the province of Ho-nan, in which Chung-mou was
situated, received word of this, he suspected it was untrue and
dispatched Fei Ch'in, the director of prisons, to go and investigate
the matter.

Lu Kung escorted Fei Ch'in here and there through the fields,
and then the two sat down together under a mulberry tree. Some
pheasants flew by and alighted close to them. A young boy was
standing nearby, and Fei Ch'in said to him, "Why don't you
catch one of them?" But the boy declined, explaining that this
was the season of the year when the pheasants were leading their
chicks. Fei Ch'in, startled by such an unexpected reply, rose from
his seat. Later, when he was taking leave of Lu Kung, he said,
"The reason I came here was so that I might observe the effects of
your administration. Now I find that the locusts have not invaded
your borders, your civilizing influence has extended to the birds
and beasts, and even little boys have learned to be kind and
compassionate – three wonders indeed!"

When he returned to his office, he drew up a report on his
findings and submitted it to the governor, Yüan An. The same
year, ears of auspicious grain were found growing in the courtyard
of the lodge where Lu Kung was staying.[1] Yüan An sent a report
of the matter to the emperor, who was duly impressed. Lu Kung
remained at his post for three years, and everyone in the region

praised his extraordinary ability. After he left the post, the officials who had worked under him recalled him with fondness. Later he was appointed minister of education. The opinions which he submitted to the throne were always based upon the Classics, and he worked behind the scenes to correct and improve the functioning of the government. But because he made no attempt to draw attention to himself, he was never singled out for commendation as a man of frankness and integrity.

Sung Chün of the Later Han, whose polite name was Shu-hsiang, was a native of An-chung in Nan-yang.

In the time of Emperor Kuang-wu [A.D. 25–57] he was assigned to the post of governor of Chiu-chiang. There were in the province many fierce tigers that frequently inflicted injury on the people. Traps and pits were constantly being constructed to catch them, but still they continued to do great harm. When Sung Chün arrived at his post, he sent out a notice to the districts under his jurisdiction which read: "Tigers and leopards live in the mountains, turtles and water lizards live in the water. Each has its natural environment. This area around the Yangtze and Huai rivers has its wild beasts just as the northern regions have their chickens and pigs. The harsh officials are the ones to blame for the injury that comes to the people. To expend all this effort setting traps and catching animals is not in accordance with the principles of concerned and compassionate government. The traps and pits should be done away with at once!" After this, it was reported that all the tigers had moved eastward and crossed over to the other side of the Yangtze.

1. "Auspicous grain" is variously defined by commentators as an unusually large variety of grain, or grain that has developed many heads. It is one of the standard omens traditionally believed to appear in response to virtuous and benevolent government, and as such was customarily reported to the throne.

37

廣 客 蛇 影

KUANG's guest – a snake reflected

殷 師 牛 鬪

YIN SHIH – bulls fighting

According to the *History of the Chin*, Yüeh Kuang, whose polite name was Yen-fu, was a native of Yü-yang in Nan-yang.

While serving as governor of Ho-nan, he had a guest who used to come to see him often and with whom he was very friendly. Abruptly, however, the man stopped coming to call. After considerable time had passed, Yüeh Kuang sent for him and inquired the reason. The guest replied, "When I was seated in your presence last, you kindly poured me a cup of wine. Just as I was about to drink it, I suddenly saw a snake in my cup. I was so revolted I could hardly get the wine down, and after drinking it I fell ill!"

At this time there was a horn-tipped bow decorated with a lacquer painting of a snake that hung on the wall of the Ho-nan government office. Yüeh Kuang realized that the snake the man had seen in his wine cup was the reflection of this bow. He therefore ordered another serving of wine placed before the man and said, "Do you see any snake in your cup this time?"

"I see the same one that was there before!" the guest replied. Yüeh Kuang then explained to him the reason, whereupon the man looked immensely relieved. After that, the illness that had troubled him for so long abruptly went away.

When Yüeh Kuang served in any particular post, he won no immediate acclaim for his administrative ability, but after he had left the assignment, the wisdom of the measures he had taken to benefit the people would become apparent and they would always remember him with fondness. In giving his opinion of others, he would invariably begin by praising the person's strong points; in this way, the person's weak points would become apparent without his having to mention them.

Later he replaced Wang Jung as chief of palace writers. Wang Jung was the one who had first recommended Yüeh Kuang for office, and the people of the time regarded it as particularly

93

appropriate that Yüeh Kuang should succeed Wang Jung in the post.

Yin Chung-k'an of the Chin dynasty was a native of Ch'en Province.

His father, Yin Shih, who served as governor of Chin-ling, was for some years troubled by illness, and Chung-k'an was so diligent in nursing him that he scarcely took the time to get out of his clothes. He began the study of the medical art himself and mastered all of its secrets and subtleties. He used to wipe the tears from his eyes while he was handling the medicine for his father, and as a result eventually lost the sight in one eye. When his father died, he observed such rigorous mourning that he all but destroyed his health, and was widely commended for his filial piety.

Emperor Hsiao-wu [A.D. 373–96] summoned him to the post of attendant to the sons of the nobility and treated him with great fondness. Yin Chung-k'an's father during his illness had been troubled by a morbidly acute sense of hearing and used to complain that the ants crawling about under his bed sounded to his ears like bulls fighting. The emperor had earlier heard the story but was unaware to whom it referred. He once said to Yin Chung-k'an, "Do you know who it was who suffered from that ailment?"

Yin Chung-k'an, tears starting from his eyes, rose from his place and, quoting a line from the *Book of Odes*, replied, "Advancing or retreating, my way is blocked!"[1] The emperor, realizing what he had done, was chagrined at his tactlessness.

Yin Chung-k'an was skilled at "pure discourse," the type of philosophical conversation popular at the time. He used to say, "If I go three days without reading Lao Tzu's discussions on the Way and its power, I feel the roots of my tongue beginning to stiffen!" He was ranked beside Han K'ang-po in his ability to discuss philosophical principles. Later he was given the imperial credentials and dispatched to put down the revolt in the region of Chiang-ling, but was pursued by the forces of Huan Hsüan, the leader of the revolt, and was forced to take his life.

1. *Ta-ya, Sang-jou,* Mao text #257; Yin means of course that he cannot bear to speak of his father's death, though it is his duty to reply to the ruler's inquiry.

38

魯褒錢神
Lu Pao – the Money God

崔烈銅臭
Ts'ui Lieh – the stink of copper

According to the *History of the Chin*, Lu Pao, whose polite name was Yüan-tao, was a native of Nan-yang.

Fond of learning and broad in knowledge, he managed, poor as he was, to make his way in the world. In the years of the *k'ang-yüan* era [A.D. 343–44] and thereafter, morals and standards of conduct declined drastically. Lu Pao, appalled by the greed and meanness that marked the age, wrote under an assumed name a work entitled "Discussion of the Money God" in which he voiced his attacks. The gist of his work was as follows:

"People love him like an elder brother, and his name is Square Hole.[1] Lose him and you are poor and weak, gain him and you are rich and flourishing. Without wings he flies, without feet he runs; he softens the sternest countenance, opens the tightest lips. The one with lots of money steps to the front, the one with only a little is shown to the rear. With money as your protector, it's 'good fortune and nothing that is not profitable!'[2]

"Why must you read books before you can be wealthy and eminent? In past times, Master Lü was delighted with an empty promise on a calling card, and Kao-tsu conquered the empire because of two hundred extra cash. Wen-chün because of it was able to doff her hemp skirt and put on brocades, and Hsiang-ju could get rid of his workman's loincloth and ride in a tall-topped carriage.[3] Office, honor, fame, eminence – all are to be had for money! Though virtueless, you may enjoy repute; though impotent, you may yet shine.[4] It opens the Golden Gate, gives entrance to the Purple Portals.[5] Through it the imperiled may be assured of safety, the doomed restored to life, the lordly brought low, and the living transformed into the dead. The proverb says, 'Money has no ears, yet it can command the gods.' To the people of today, it is money alone that counts!"

Those who were grieved by the conditions of the time copied the piece and handed it about, but what became of Lu Pao after that, no one knows.

Ts'ui Lieh of the Later Han was a native of An-p'ing in Cho Province. He enjoyed wide repute in the northern regions and, after serving as the governor of various provinces, advanced to one of the nine highest posts in the government.

In the reign of Emperor Ling [A.D. 168–88] the government opened up the Hung-tu Gate office, hanging up placards announcing the sale of official posts and ranks in the nobility, each assigned a specific price, from the most exalted on down. The richest people were allowed to come forward with their money first, and when the less affluent had purchased offices, they often discovered later that they had to pay double the fixed rate. There were others who preferred a different route, working through attendants in the palace or the wet nurses at court to gain advancement. At this time various men such as Tuan Chiung were granted honors and titles and enjoyed great repute, but all were obliged to hand over large amounts of money and goods before they could ascend to such heights. Ts'ui Lieh, enlisting the aid of one of the wet nurses, paid five million cash in exchange for the office of minister of education.[6]

He once questioned his son Chün, saying, "Now that I am ranked among the three highest ministers, what sort of opinion do people have of me?"

Chün replied, "When you were young, father, you were very well spoken of, and you advanced in rank from governor to an important post in the central government. People at that time used to say that it was only right you should in time hold one of the three highest posts. But now that you have advanced to that height, the world is greatly disappointed."

"Why should that be?" asked Ts'ui Lieh.

Chün replied, "What they don't like about it, they say, is the stink of copper!"

Later Ts'ui Lieh was appointed grand commandant. After the rebel Tung Cho had been put to death, he was honored with the title of commander of the city gate.

1. A reference to the square holes in traditional Chinese coins.
2. An imitation of the language of the *Book of Changes*.
3. When Kao-tsu, the founder of the Han, was still poor and unknown, he

joined a party for a distinguished visitor named Master Lü, sending in a calling card with a completely empty promise of a gift of ten thousand cash. Master Lü welcomed him and aided him to power. Around the same time, Kao-tsu was sent off on a labor party. Hsiao Ho, a local official, gave him a parting gift of five hundred cash, two hundred more than any of the other officials presented. Hsiao Ho later became a trusted aid to Kao-tsu and helped him win control of the empire. The poet Ssu-ma Hsiang-ju eloped with Wen-chün, daughter of a wealthy family, and for a time the couple endured great poverty, but they were eventually forgiven and were able to live in style; see p. 155.
4. The last is a jibe at the court eunuchs, who often wielded great power.
5. The gates of the imperial palace.
6. The *ssu-t'u* or minister of education (sometimes translated minister of the masses) had originally been only one of six high government posts, but by this time the office had virtually replaced that of prime minister in importance.

39

陵母伏劍

WANG LING's mother falls on a sword

軻親斷機

MENG K'o's mother cuts the thread

Wang Ling of the Former Han was a native of P'ei. At the time Kao-tsu, the founder of the Han, began his uprising, Wang Ling also gathered together a band of several thousand followers. When Kao-tsu attacked Hsiang Yü, his chief rival, Wang Ling placed his followers under the command of Kao-tsu, who at this time held the title of king of Han.

Hsiang Yü seized Wang Ling's mother and held her captive in the midst of his camp. When an envoy arrived from Wang Ling, Hsiang Yü seated Wang Ling's mother in the place of honor facing east, hoping by such favorable treatment to induce Wang Ling to come over to his side. As the envoy was leaving, Wang Ling's mother, who had come to take leave of him in private, wept and said, "There is something I want you to tell my son for me. Let him serve the king of Han with all diligence, for the king of Han is a worthy man. He must not be of two minds on my account! See, I send off his envoy with the gift of my death!" And with this she fell upon a sword and died.

According to the old *Lieh-nü-chuan* or *Biographies of Outstanding Women*,[1] the mother of Meng K'o or Mencius of Tsou lived in a house near a graveyard. When Mencius was little, he used to play games that imitated the ceremonies conducted in the graveyard. "This is no place for me to bring up a son," his mother said, and moved out, taking a house beside the marketplace. This time Mencius played at hawking wares in the manner of the merchants. Once more his mother said, "This is no place for my son to live," and moved again, this time to a house beside a school. In his games Mencius thereupon set up sacrificial stands and vessels and imitated the ritual bowings and polite yieldings that he saw the students practicing. "This is the right place for my son!" said his mother, and made her home there.

In time Mencius himself went off to school. When he came

home, his mother asked if he was making progress in his studies. "Nothing special," replied Mencius. His mother then took a knife and cut the thread of the loom on which she was weaving. "For you to neglect your studies is the same as for me to cut the thread of my weaving!" Mencius was very startled and after that applied himself morning and evening to his studies without rest. He studied under Tzu-ssu and in time became a famous Confucian scholar.[2] Gentlemen of perception, observing Mencius's mother, said, "She knows the right way to be a mother."

1. A work compiled by Liu Hsiang (77–6 B.C.) of the Former Han. Hsü designates it "old" to distinguish it from later imitations of the work.
2. Tzu-ssu was a grandson of Confucius; the more common account is that Mencius studied under a disciple of Tzu-ssu.

Hu Wei hands over the silk

Lu Chi hides the oranges

According to the *History of the Chin*, Hu Wei, whose polite name was Po-wu, was a native of Shou-ch'un in Huai-nan.

His father Hu Chih was noted for his loyalty and integrity and served as provincial director of Ching Province under the Wei dynasty. Hu Wei, who was pursuing his studies in the capital, once made a trip home to see how his father was faring. Since the family was poor, he had no horse or carriage or grooms to attend him, but made the trip alone, trotting along on a donkey. After reaching home and visiting with his father, he prepared to return to the capital, whereupon his father presented him with a bolt of silk. "Father, I know your integrity and high ideals," said Hu Wei. "How did you happen to acquire a piece of silk like this?"

"I bought it with some of my official salary I had left over," his father replied.

Hu Wei accepted the gift and took his leave, but eventually he gave the silk to the military supervisor serving on his father's staff. Later he himself became provincial director of Hsü Province, applying himself diligently to the art of administration and bringing about a vast improvement in the morals and customs of the area under his jurisdiction.

Once, when he was attending court, Emperor Wu [A.D. 265–89] asked him, "Who excels in integrity, you or your father?"

Hu Wei replied, "My father worries that other people may learn of his integrity, I worry that they won't. I come nowhere near equaling him!"

According to the *Account of Wu*, Lu Chi, whose polite name was Kung-chi, was a native of Wu.

At the age of six, he had an opportunity to meet Yüan Shu, who at the time controlled the region of Chiu-chiang. Yüan Shu put out some oranges for him to eat. Lu Chi surreptitiously stuffed three of them into the breast of his robe, but when he was making his parting bows, they fell to the ground. "Master Lu," said Yüan Shu, "is it proper for a guest to be hiding oranges in the breast of his robe?"

Lu Chi knelt down and said, "I only wanted to take them home to give to my mother!" Yüan Shu was much struck by his action.

Lu Chi was a man of broad learning and understanding, and had read all the extant works on astronomy and mathematics. Sun Ch'üan [A.D. 222–51], the ruler of Wu, appointed him to a post in the central government, but he aroused disfavor by his outspokenness. He was dispatched from the capital and sent to serve as governor of Yü-lin, at the same time being appointed a subordinate general. But his interest lay in Confucianism and scholarship and he had no desire for a career as a general. Thus, although he attended to his military duties, he continued his literary labors as in the past. He devised a diagram illustrating the *Hun-t'ien* or ecliptical theory of the universe, and wrote a commentary on the *Book of Changes* and expositions of the philosophy of Lao Tzu, all of which circulated among the people of the period.

41

西施捧心
Hsi Shih pounds her breast

孫壽折腰
Sun Shou sways her hips

The *Chuang Tzu* says: Hsi Shih, troubled with heartburn, frowned at her neighbors. An ugly woman of the neighborhood, seeing that Hsi Shih was beautiful, went home and likewise pounded her breast and frowned at her neighbors. She understood that someone frowning could be beautiful, but she did not understand where the beauty of the frown came from.

Hsi Shih was a woman of Yüeh and is often referred to as Hsi Tzu. Her beauty was unmatched among the women of her time. King Kou-chien of Yüeh presented her to his rival, King Fu-ch'a of Wu. King Fu-ch'a became completely infatuated with her, and in the end his kingdom was overthrown [472 B.C.].

Liang Chi was a general in chief of the Later Han. His wife Sun Shou was enfeoffed as Lady of Hsiang-ch'eng and in addition was granted the privilege of wearing red leather knee-guards, enjoying honors equal to those of an elder princess of the imperial family. Sun Shou was very beautiful and skilled at affecting seductive ways. She would paint her face with "melancholy eyebrows," put teardrop makeup under her eyes, wear her hair in a "falling-horse" coiffure, affect a "swaying-hip" walk and a smile that looked as though she were suffering from a toothache, all in order to enhance her charm and attractiveness. By nature she was as tenacious as a pair of tweezers and managed to dominate her husband completely. As a result he treated her with great favor but at the same time lived in awe of her. Eventually, when Liang Chi fell from power, she joined him in committing suicide [A.D. 159].

42

靈 輒 扶 輪
LING CH'E supports the wheel

魏 顆 結 草
WEI K'O knots the grasses

According to the *Tso chuan*, Duke Ling [620–607 B.C.] of the state of Chin did not conduct himself in the manner of a proper ruler. Chao Hsüan-tzu repeatedly remonstrated with him. The duke, much annoyed, invited Hsüan-tzu to a drinking party and had soldiers concealed nearby, intending to do away with him. The duke set his mastiff on Hsüan-tzu, but Shih Mi-ming, the attendant who rode with Hsüan-tzu in his carriage at his right side, struck the dog and killed it. Hsüan-tzu said, "You discard men and employ a dog, but fierce as it is, what can it do!" Fighting his way along, Hsüan-tzu managed to escape, but Shih Mi-ming was killed in the fray.

Once in the past Hsüan-tzu had gone hunting to Shou Mountain and had encamped under a shady mulberry. There he discovered Ling Ch'e, an official of Chin, who had not eaten for three days and was starving. Hsüan-tzu gave him some food, but he ate only half and put the rest aside. When Hsüan-tzu asked him the reason, he replied, "I have been serving as an official in the capital for three years and I do not know whether my mother is still alive or not. But now that I have come this far and am near my home, I want to save the rest of the food to take to her." Hsüan-tzu instructed him to finish the meal, and meanwhile had a box of rice and some meat prepared for him which he put into a bag and gave to him.

Later, Ling Ch'e became a guard in the service of the duke. When the duke ordered his men to attack Hsüan-tzu, Ling Ch'e turned and faced the duke's men with his spear, holding them off while Hsüan-tzu made his escape. When Hsüan-tzu asked him the reason, he replied, "I was the starving man in the shade of the mulberry." Hsüan-tzu tried to inquire his name and place of residence, but Ling Ch'e would say nothing further and disappeared. Hsüan-tzu also fled from the capital.[1]

According to the *Tso chuan*, Wei K'o of the state of Chin was the son of Wei Wu-tzu. Wei Wu-tzu had a favorite concubine who had borne him no children. Falling ill, he gave orders to his son, saying, "After I am gone, see that she is provided with a husband." When his illness grew more severe, however, he said, "Make certain that she is put to death and buried with me!" At length, when he died, his son Wei K'o arranged for the concubine to be married, saying, "When the illness was severe, my father's mind became deranged. I abide by the orders he gave when his mind was still clear."

Later, when an army from Ch'in invaded Chin [594 B.C.], Wei K'o defeated it at Fu-shih and captured Tu Hui, a warrior of Ch'in noted for his great strength. While the battle was still in progress, Wei K'o saw an old man tying the grasses together in such a way as to block Tu Hui's way. Tu Hui stumbled over the grasses and fell to the ground, thus making it possible for Wei K'o to capture him. That night the old man appeared to Wei K'o in a dream and said, "I am the father of the woman you gave away in marriage. You followed the orders which your honored father gave when he was still in his right mind. I have done this to repay you."[2]

1. It will be noted that Hsü's commentary, which follows the account in the *Tso chuan*, fails to explain the supporting of the wheel mentioned in the *Meng Ch'iu* couplet. Versions of the tale found in earlier commentaries record that when Hsüan-tzu tried to escape in his carriage, he found that the duke's men had removed one of its wheels. Ling Ch'e thereupon lifted up the axle with his arms and, taking the place of the missing wheel, made it possible for Hsüan-tzu to flee from the scene in his carriage.
2. Wei K'o's action is often cited to support the contention that a parent's commands are to be followed not blindly but with discretion.

43

滄臺毀璧
TAN T'AI destroys a jade

子罕辭寶
TZU-HAN declines a treasure

According to the *Po-wu-chih* or *Record of Diverse Things*, Tan T'ai, whose polite name was Tzu-yü, was once crossing the Yellow River with a jade disc worth a thousand pieces of gold. The River Lord, god of the river, decided he wanted the jade and thereupon caused fierce waves to rise up, sending two dragons to press upon the boat from either side. Tan T'ai, holding the jade disc in his left hand, drew his sword with his right hand and slashed at the dragons, killing them both. Having reached the opposite shore, however, he then threw the jade into the river, but the River Lord leaped up and tossed it back to him, an action that was repeated three times. Tan T'ai thereupon smashed the disc to bits and went on his way.[1]

According to the *Tso chuan*, a man of the state of Sung acquired a piece of jade which he wished to present to the minister of works Yüeh Tzu-han, but the latter refused to accept it. The man presenting the jade said, "I have shown it to a jade expert and he assures me it is a real treasure – therefore I am presenting it to you!"

Yüeh Tzu-han said, "You look on jade as a treasure, I look on lack of greed as a treasure. If you give it to me, we will both be losing our treasures. Men do better to hold on to the treasures they have."

1. In this curious anecdote the reader is left to surmise the motives behind the apparently contradictory actions of Tan T'ai and the River Lord.

44

田單火牛

T'IEN TAN sets fire to the oxen

江逌燕雞

CHIANG YÜ lights the chickens

According to the *Shih chi* or *Records of the Historian*, T'ien Tan was a member of one of the remoter branches of the great T'ien family of the state of Ch'i. He served as a marketplace official in Lin-tzu, the Ch'i capital, but failed to attract any special notice.

When the state of Yen dispatched Yüeh Yi to attack and smash the Ch'i forces [284 B.C.], nearly all the cities of Ch'i were forced to surrender. T'ien Tan, however, managed to escape and fled east to Chi-mo, one of the few cities that continued to hold out. When the men of Yen pressed their attack on Chi-mo, T'ien Tan rounded up a thousand or more oxen from within the city and had them fitted with coverings of red silk on which dragon shapes had been painted in five colors. He tied knives to their horns and bundles of grease-soaked reeds to their tails and then, setting fire to their tails, drove them out into the night through some twenty or thirty openings which had been tunneled in the city wall. Five thousand of the best soldiers poured out after them.

The oxen, maddened by the fires that burned their tails, rushed into the Yen encampment which, it being night, was filled with terror. Wherever the Yen soldiers looked, they saw nothing but dragon shapes, and all who stood within the path of the oxen were wounded or killed. The five thousand soldiers, gags in their mouths so they would make no noise, moved forward to attack, while from within the city came an accompaniment of drumming and clamor, the old men and boys all beating on bronze vessels to make a noise until the sound of it shook heaven and earth. The Yen army was completely defeated, and in time all of Ch'i's seventy or more cities were restored to Ch'i rule. A party was sent to Chü, where the royal family had fled, and a new ruler, King Hsiang, was put on the throne of Ch'i. The king enfeoffed T'ien Tan with the title of lord of An-p'ing.

Chiang Yu of the Chin, whose polite name was Tao-tsai, was a native of Yü in Ch'en-liu.

The general of the middle army Yin Hao requested that he be appointed as an army consultant; later he was transferred to the post of chief clerk. At this time the Ch'iang and Ting-ling tribes had risen in revolt [A.D. 353] and Yin Hao's forces were filled with alarm and terror. Yao Hsiang, the leader of the Ch'iang, made his camp a mere ten *li* away from Yin Hao and was pressing hard on him. Yin Hao ordered Chiang Yu to attack. Chiang Yu accordingly led his men and advanced to Yao Hsiang's camp. "It's not that our men are not well trained," he said to his officers. "But the Ch'iang greatly outnumber us and their stockades and fortifications are so solidly built that they would be very difficult to take by force. I have a scheme, however, whereby I think we can overcome the enemy!"

He then gathered several hundred chickens and tied them all together with a long rope. This done, he attached fires to their feet and turned them loose. The chickens in their alarm attempted to scatter and, flying up into the air, came down in the midst of Yao Hsiang's encampment. Soon the camp was in flames and Chiang Yu, taking advantage of the ensuing confusion, launched his attack. In the end Yao Hsiang suffered a temporary setback. Chiang Yu was later transferred to the post of master of ritual.

45

陳 平 多 轍
CH'EN P'ING – many wheel tracks

李 廣 成 蹊
LI KUANG – a well-beaten path

Ch'en P'ing of the Former Han was a native of Hu-yu in Yang-wu. When he was young his family was very poor. He loved to read books and studied the teachings of Lao Tzu and the Yellow Emperor. He was tall and very good-looking. In time he reached the age for taking a wife. But none of the wealthy families was willing to offer him their daughter, and he was too proud to marry a girl from a poor family, so the years passed and he remained single.

There was a rich old woman named Chang whose grand-daughter had been married five times, but each time her husband had immediately died.[1] As a result, no one dared to take her as a wife. Ch'en P'ing, however, decided that he wanted to marry her. The old woman, impressed by Ch'en P'ing's good looks, once followed him to his house. His home was at the far end of a lane and backed against the outer wall of the city, with only some old worn matting hung up for a doorway. Yet outside the door were many tracks made by the sort of carriages ridden in by people of means.

When the old woman returned to her own home, she said to her son Chung, "I wish to marry my granddaughter to Ch'en P'ing."

"Ch'en P'ing is poor and does nothing to earn a living," Chung objected. "Throughout the whole district people just laugh at his ways. Why should you want to marry this girl to him?"

"Anyone as good-looking as Ch'en P'ing will never stay poor for long," said the old lady, and in the end she gave him the girl for a wife. She provided the supplies of wine and meat for the wedding celebration and cautioned her granddaughter, saying, "You must never be inattentive in serving your husband just because he is poor!"

Ch'en P'ing was made steward of the local shrine. He divided the meat from the sacrifices among the worshippers with such fairness that the elders all praised him. Ch'en P'ing said, "If I could become steward of the empire, I would divide it up in the same way as this meat!"

Later he became a follower of Kao-tsu, the founder of the Han dynasty, and having been appointed colonel of the guard had supervision over all the other generals. Kao-tsu gave Ch'en P'ing a sum of forty thousand catties of yellow gold to use as he wished, making no further inquiry about the matter.[2] Ch'en P'ing used a large part of the money to create dissension among the forces of Kao-tsu's rival, Hsiang Yü of Ch'u. From the time he joined Kao-tsu until the empire was finally conquered, Ch'en P'ing devised a total of six ingenious strategies to assist Kao-tsu. After the founding of the Han, he was enfeoffed as marquis of Ch'ü-ni. In the reign of Emperor Hui he served as chancellor of the left, and under Empress Lü as chancellor of the right. He also served as chancellor under Emperor Wen before his death [178 B.C.].

Li Kuang of the Former Han was a native of Ch'eng-chi in Lung-hsi. The art of archery had been handed down in his family for generations.

Li Kuang was out hunting one time when he spied a rock in the grass which he mistook for a tiger. He shot an arrow at the rock and hit it with such force that the tip of the arrow embedded itself in the rock. Later he discovered that it was a rock, but another day when he tried shooting at it again, he was unable to pierce it.

In the time of Emperor Wu he was appointed governor of the border province of Yu-pei-p'ing. The Hsiung-nu tribes referred to him as "The Flying General of the Han" and stayed away from the region for several years, not daring to cross the frontier.

Li Kuang served as the governor of seven provinces in succession over a period of more than forty years. Whenever he received a reward of some kind, he at once divided it among those in his command, and he was content to eat and drink the same things as his men. He was very lenient with his men and did nothing to vex them, so that they were happy to serve under him.

During the *yuan-shou* era [122–117 B.C.] he was appointed general of the vanguard and joined the general in chief Wei Ch'ing in an attack on the Hsiung-nu, but he became confused and lost his way in the desert. Wei Ch'ing, wishing to submit a report to the emperor explaining why the army had gone astray, sent his chief clerk to reprimand Li Kuang and order him to report to general headquarters to answer a list of charges that had been drawn up against him. Li Kuang said to his officers, "Since I was old enough to wear my hair bound up, I have fought over seventy engagements, large and small, with the Hsiung-nu. But this time I lost my way. Heaven must have planned it like this! Now I am over sixty – much too old to stand up to a bunch of petty clerks!" Then he drew his sword and cut his throat. When word of this reached the common people, those who had known him and those who had not, old men and young boys alike, were all moved to tears by his fate.

The appraisal says:[3] General Li Kuang was a man so simple and sincere that one would take him for a peasant, and almost incapable of speaking a word. And yet the day he died all the people of the empire, whether they had known him or not, were moved to the profoundest grief, so deeply did men trust his sincerity. There is a proverb that says, "Though the peach tree does not speak, the world wears a path beneath it." It is a small saying, but one which is capable of conveying a great meaning.

1. Some commentators take Chang to be a rich old man named Chang Fu. Whether a grandmother or grandfather, the person would, according to Confucian custom, have the right to decide upon a grandchild's marriage.
2. The text reads "four million catties," but this is an error; I follow the reading in Ch'en's biography in *Shih chi* 56 and *Han shu* 50.
3. The *tsan* or appraisal section with which the biography of Li Kuang in *Han shu* 54 concludes; it is taken verbatim from Ssu-ma Ch'ien's biography of Li Kuang in *Shih chi* 109.

46

龔 勝 不 屈

Kung Sheng refuses to give in

孫 寶 自 劾

Sun Pao has himself dismissed

Kung Sheng of the Former Han, whose polite name was Chün-pin, and Kung She, whose polite name was Chün-ch'ien, were natives of the region of Ch'u. They were good friends, and were both noted for their integrity. People of the time referred to them as the Two Kungs of Ch'u.

In the time of Emperor Ai [6 B.C.–A.D. 1] Kung Sheng was appointed counselor to the keeper of the palace gate. When Wang Mang began to usurp the powers of government, Kung Sheng asked to be dismissed and allowed to retire to his home. Wang Mang later sent messengers to his home offering to appoint him director of educational affairs, but Kung Sheng declined on grounds of illness. Still later, Wang Mang, who by this time had overthrown the Han and made himself emperor of a new dynasty, once more sent messengers bearing a letter with the imperial seal and the seal cords of the post of tutor to the heir apparent. These were offered to Kung Sheng, along with a comfortable carriage drawn by four horses to carry him to the capital.

The governor of the province, the chief clerks of the districts, subordinate officials and scholars of the region, over a thousand persons in all, journeyed to Kung Sheng's home to be present at the delivery of the imperial summons. Kung Sheng, protesting that he was too ill to rise from his bed, lay with his head facing east, the proper position for a minister when receiving the visit of his lord, and had his court robes laid over him and his sash draped on top of them. "I received generous honors from the house of Han," he said, "and have been unable to repay them. Now I am old and at any moment may go to my grave. How could it be right for one man to serve the rulers of two different dynasties! I will go to the world below to greet my former lord!" Having finished speaking, he refused thereafter to open his mouth to take food or drink, and at the end of fourteen days died.

Kung She was an expert in the Five Classics and was appointed governor of T'ai-shan, but after a few months he asked to be dismissed and allowed to return home. Emperor Ai sent messengers to his home offering him the post of counselor to the keeper of the palace gate and several times granted him permission to delay the assumption of his duties, but in the end he refused to accept the appointment. After Kung Sheng and Kung She had left their posts and were living at home, the two-thousand-picul officials and chief clerks who had newly been appointed to office invariably went to their homes to pay respects, conducting themselves with the courtesy appropriate to disciples in the presence of their teacher.

Sun Pao of the Former Han, whose polite name was Tzu-yen, was a native of Yen-ling in Ying-ch'uan.

Having qualified as an "expert in the Classics," he was made a provincial official. The imperial secretary Chang Chung, however, assigned him to a post in his own office, intending to employ him to tutor his son in the Classics. Sun Pao thereupon had himself impeached and dismissed from office. Later, he took a position as a lowly secretary and moved into the quarters assigned to such officials. Chang Chung, puzzled by such action, sent a close friend to question him.

"Formerly," said the friend, "His Lordship provided you with very imposing lodgings, yet you had yourself impeached and left the assignment, presumably because you wished to demonstrate your high sense of integrity. The lofty-minded gentlemen in the offices of the imperial secretary and the chancellor would ordinarily consider it beneath their dignity to serve as a mere secretary, and yet you have accepted such a post, moved into the official lodgings, and appear to be completely happy. Is this not inconsistent with your former behavior?"

Sun Pao replied, "A lofty-minded gentleman, it is true, would not serve as a secretary. But His Lordship has given me permission to hold such a post, and the rest of the officials in his office have no right to criticize. Why should a man be so concerned about showing off his lofty-mindedness? Some time ago, however, because His Lordship's son wanted to study literature, I was transferred to a post at His Lordship's side. According to ritual, the student comes to study with the teacher; it is not proper that the

112

teacher should have to go to the student! The Way cannot be humbled, but humbling the body – what harm does that do? If one is not fortunate enough to encounter a man who truly appreciates him, then he may have to accept any type of assignment at all. Certainly acting as a secretary is no great problem!"

When Chang Chung received word of the interview, he was much chagrined and submitted a letter to the throne recommending Sun Pao. During the reign of Emperor P'ing [A.D. 1–5], Sun Pao became minister of agriculture.

47

呂安題鳳
Lü An writes the word "Phoenix"

子猷尋戴
Tzu-yu sets off to visit Tai

According to the *Shih-shuo hsin-yü* or *New Specimens of Contemporary Talk*, Hsi K'ang and Lü An were very close friends, and if one of them took it into his head to visit the other, he would call for his carriage and ride a thousand *li* to do so. Once Lü An arrived at Hsi K'ang's house after the latter had gone out. Hsi K'ang's elder brother Hsi came to the door to greet him. Lü An declined to enter, however, but simply wrote the word "Phoenix" on the gate and went on his way. Hsi was not sure what to make of this, but took it as a compliment. He failed to consider that the character for "phoenix," when taken apart, is found to be composed of the characters for "common" and "fowl."

Wang Hui-chih of the Chin, whose polite name was Tzu-yu, was a son of the general of the right Wang Hsi-chih. He was a man of highly unusual temperament who refused to bow to convention. He served as a staff officer under the grand marshal Huan Wen, but went around with his hair in a tangle and his sash untied and took no heed of official business. He was once staying for a short time in a vacant house, but nevertheless immediately had bamboos planted in the garden. When someone asked why he bothered, he merely gave a long drawn-out whistle and then, pointing to the bamboos, said, "How could I do without these gentlemen for even a day!"

He was once living in the district of Shan-yin. One evening, after a snowfall, the sky cleared and the moon shone clear and bright, turning eveything in all four directions into an expanse of white. Wang Hui-chih sat alone, pouring wine for himself and intoning Tso Ssu's poem "Invitation to Hiding,"[1] when he suddenly remembered his recluse friend Tai K'uei. Tai K'uei was at this time living in the nearby district of Shan. Though it was already night, Wang Hui-chih immediately set out in a little boat to visit him, arriving in Shan the following morning. But when he got as far as Tai K'uei's gate, he went no farther; instead, he turned around and started home again. Asked the reason, he replied, "I set off on the trip on an impulse, and when the impulse came to an end, I turned around. Why was there any need for me to see Tai K'uei?"

In official life he advanced to the post of attendant of the Yellow Gate.

1. A poem by Tso Ssu (A.D. 250?–305?) which describes the delights of the life of the recluse. Wang Hui-chih's father was the famous calligrapher Wang Hsi-chih (A.D. 303–79).

48

蘇韶鬼靈

Su Shao's departed spirit

盧充幽婚

Lu Ch'ung's ghostly wedding

According to the *Spring and Autumn Annals of the Thirty States*, after Su Shao, the magistrate of the district of Chung-mou, had died, his cousin Chieh one day encountered him riding around on a horse in the middle of the day. His hair was tied up in a black turban and he was wearing an unlined yellow robe. Chieh took the opportunity to inquire about the spirit world.

Su Shao replied, "Dead people become ghosts and together go wandering around heaven and earth. They are here in the world of men, but they have no dealings with the living. Confucius's disciples Yen Hui and Pu Shang are at present acting as the officials in charge of education. Generally speaking, there's little difference between the living and the dead. The dead are formless, the living have substance – that's the only difference." When he had finished speaking, he disappeared from view.

The old commentaries on the *Meng Ch'iu* quote a work called *K'ung-shih chih-kuai* or *Mister K'ung's Record of Wonders*, which tells of one Lu Ch'ung of the Han, a native of Fan-yang. Forty *li* west of his house was the tomb of the daughter of the privy treasurer Ts'ui. Lu Ch'ung once went hunting in the vicinity and was pursuing a roe deer when suddenly he spied the vermilion gates of an official lodge. A man came out to greet him and took him in to see the privy treasurer Ts'ui, who said, "I recently received a letter from your honored father asking me to give you my youngest daughter for a wife. That is why I have summoned you." Ts'ui then took out a letter and showed it to him, and it was indeed in the handwriting of his deceased father.

Ts'ui then ordered his daughter to put on her makeup and adornments in the eastern chamber, led Lu Ch'ung into the presence of the bride, and performed the wedding ceremony. Lu Ch'ung remained there for three days, and when he was about to take his departure, Ts'ui said to him, "Your wife is pregnant.

If she should give birth to a boy, I will see that he is turned over to you." Then he presented Lu Ch'ung with clothes and articles of bedding and ordered a carriage to take him home.

Three years after returning home, Lu Ch'ung was enjoying the outing on the banks of a river that was customarily held on the third day of the third month when he suddenly spied two bullock carts coming over the water, now sinking, now bobbing into view again until at last they reached the shore. Peering into the carts, Lu Ch'ung saw his wife of the Ts'ui family riding in one of them with a little three-year-old boy, while in the other was the privy treasurer Ts'ui. Ts'ui took the child in his arms and handed him to Lu Ch'ung along with a poem and a golden bowl, and then the group abruptly vanished from sight. When the boy grew up, he served as the governor of serveral different provinces in succession.

49

CHEN fears the four who know

秉去三惑

PING shuns the three that mislead

Yang Chen of the Later Han, having been recommended as a man of outstanding talent, was four times appointed provincial director of Ching. Later, when he was on his way to take up the post of governor of Tung-lai, he happened to pass through Ch'ang-i. The magistrate of Ch'ang-i was one Wang Mi of Ching, a man whom Yang Chen had earlier recommended for his outstanding talent. Wang Mi paid a call on Yang Chen and, when evening came, took a gift of ten catties of gold out of the breast of his robe and presented it to Yang Chen. Yang Chen said, "I believe I know what kind of man you are. How is it that you don't know what kind of man I am?"

"Twilight has fallen," said Wang Mi. "No one will ever know about it!"

But Yang Chen replied, "Heaven will know, the spirits will know, I will know, you will know – how can you say no one will know about it!"

Wang Mi, much chagrined, took his departure. This was the kind of public-spirited and scrupulous character that Yang Chen possessed, refusing to countenance such interviews of a private nature. As a result, his sons and grandsons ate simple fare and went about on foot. An old friend of his wanted to help him open up some kind of business enterprise, but Yang Chen refused, saying, "I want people in later ages to speak of my sons and grandsons as the descendants of an honest and upright official. This will be my legacy to them – a generous one, if I may say so!"

In the time of Emperor An [A.D. 107–125] he served as grand commandant but was slandered by the gentleman in constant attendance Fan Feng and eventually committed suicide.

Yang Ping of the Later Han, whose polite name was Shu-chieh, was the second son of Yang Chen. During the time of Emperor Huan [A.D. 147–67] he served as grand commandant. Whenever he detected faults or abuses at court, he would immediately speak out in a spirit of unfailing loyalty, doing his best to correct them, and his advice was on many occasions heeded. He was by nature a man who never drank wine, and in addition he lost his wife at an early age and never remarried. As a result, he was everywhere praised for his purity of conduct. He himself always used to say, "There are three things that can never lead me astray – wine, sex, and money."

50

孫康映雪
SUN K'ANG borrows the light of the snow

車胤聚螢
CH'E YIN gathers fireflies

According to the *Sun-shih shih-lu* or *Genealogical Records of the Sun Clan*, Sun K'ang of the Chin came from a family too poor to buy oil for lamps; therefore, on winter nights he always read by the moonlight reflected on the snow. From youth he was pure and upright in character and had no dealings with those who were not. Later he advanced to the position of imperial secretary.

Ch'e Yin of the Chin, whose polite name was Wu-tzu, was a native of Nan-p'ing.

Diligent and tireless, he in time became a man of broad knowledge and understanding. His family was often too poor to buy oil for lamps, and so in the summer months he would fill a gauze bag with several dozen fireflies and use it to light his books, thus continuing his studies far into the night.

When Huan Wen held office in the province of Ching, he selected Ch'e Yin to serve on his staff, placing great trust in him because of his clear understanding of principles. Ch'e Yin gradually advanced until he held the post of chief clerk to the general of the western campaign, and eventually became known at court. At that time he and Wu Yin-chih were both famed as men who, in spite of poverty and hardship, had managed to acquire great learning. He was also skillful at mingling in society, and whenever there was a gathering of guests, if he did not happen to be present, people would all say, "How can we possibly enjoy ourselves without Lord Ch'e!" At the time of his death he held the post of head of the board of civil affairs.

51

谷永筆札

KU YUNG's brush and writing tablet

顧愷丹青

KU K'AI-CHIH's red and green pigments

Ku Yung of the Former Han, whose polite name was Tzu-yün, was a native of Ch'ang-an. He and Lou Hu were both chief retainers of the Five Marquises of the powerful Wang clan. In Ch'ang-an people would speak of "the brush and writing tablet of Ku Yung and the lips and tongue of Lou Hu," meaning that these could be trusted and used to good effect.

Ku Yung had a very broad and thorough knowledge of the Classics and other works of literature, ranking with such scholars as Tu Ch'in and Tu Yeh, though he could not match the erudition of Liu Hsiang and his son Liu Hsin, nor of Yang Hsiung. He was particularly well informed on the "Heavenly Offices" section of the *Rites of Chou* and the Ching Fang version of the *Book of Changes* and therefore was expert in interpreting omens and portents. The last post he held was that of minister of agriculture.

Lou Hu's polite name was Chün-ch'ing. In his youth he joined his father in the practice of medicine, coming and going in the houses of the nobles and relatives of the emperor. At this time the Wang family was at the zenith of its power and guests and retainers filled its gates. The Five Marquises, all brothers of the Wang clan, competed for fame. Retainers of the five customarily had a single household at which they were supported and were not permitted to pass back and forth from one household to another; only Lou Hu was received at the homes of all five marquises, for everywhere he had won acceptance. He was clever in argumentation and always reasoned in accordance with honor and justice so that his listeners all respected him. In official service he rose to the post of governor of Kuang-han. When Wang Mang usurped the powers of government, he summoned Lou Hu to take charge of the region of Ch'ien-hui-kuang.

According to the *Hsi-ching tsa-chi* or *Miscellaneous Notes on the Western Capital*, the Five Marquises vied with one another in serving rare and unusual dishes at their tables. Lou Hu combined various of these ingredients to produce a kind of fish and meat dish which became known as "Five Marquis Stew" and was widely praised for its delicious flavor.

Ku K'ai-chih of the Chin, whose polite name was Ch'ang-k'ang, was a native of Wu-hsi in Chin-ling, a man of broad learning and talent.

He loved to joke, and many people as a result treated him with familiarity and affection. Whenever he ate sugarcane, he would start at the rather flavorless tip and work down toward the base. When someone asked him the reason for this strange procedure, he replied, "I like to ease into the good part gradually."

Ku K'ai-chih excelled in painting, his sketches from life being especially marvelous. Once he filled a box with his paintings, sealed and labeled it, and left it in the care of Huan Wen, under whom he was serving as an official. The works in the box were all ones he particularly prized. Huan Wen contrived to remove the back of the box and steal them, after which he glued the box back together as it had been and returned it to Ku K'ai-chih, remarking that it had never been opened. Ku K'ai-chih saw that the seal and label were untouched, and when he found that the box was empty, he immediately exclaimed, "My paintings are so wonderful they have moved the gods, who have transformed them and spirited them away! They're just like those men who turn into immortals!" He never once displayed the faintest sign of suspicion. The young people of the time admired him for the way in which he passed off the incident by absurdly boasting of his skill, and regarded the whole thing as a great joke.

When he first took a post in Huan Wen's office, Huan Wen once remarked, "Ku K'ai-chih's body is made up half of stupidity and half of cleverness. Appraising the combination, I'd have to say it achieves a perfect balance!" As a result, it became customary to speak of Ku K'ai-chih as a man of three superb qualities – superb talent, superb skill as a painter, and superb stupidity. At the time of his death [A.D. 402] he held the post of assistant to the gentlemen in constant attendance and supplementary cavalrymen.

52

戴逵破琴

TAI K'UEI smashes his lute

謝敷應星

HSIEH FU responds to the stars

According to the *History of the Chin*, Tai K'uei, whose polite name was An-tao, was a native of Ch'iao-kuo.

From the time of his youth he was widely learned, gifted in composition, skilled at playing the lute, a talented painter and calligrapher, and a master of all the other arts as well. Ssu-ma Hsi, the prince of Wu-ling and son of Emperor Yüan [A.D. 317–22], heard of his skill at lute-playing and sent a messenger to summon him. Tai K'uei confronted the messenger, smashed his lute to bits, and announced, "Tai An-tao is not a hired musician in the service of any prince!" The prince was enraged and sent a summons to Tai K'uei's elder brother Tai Shu. Tai Shu, delighted, immediately picked up his lute and hurried to obey. In the years that followed, Tai K'uei was repeatedly invited to take office but he refused to comply.

Hsieh Fu of the Chin, whose polite name was Ch'ing-hsü, was a native of K'uai-chi.

Pure and tranquil by nature, with few desires, he retired to the T'ai-p'ing Mountains and lived there over ten years, refusing all invitations to enter official life. Once the new moon strayed into the constellation known as Shao-wei.[1] One of the stars in Shao-wei is named the Hermit Star, and the diviners therefore interpreted the event as portending something that would befall a recluse. At this time the recluse Tai K'uei of the province of Wu was noted for his outstanding talent, and people began to worry about his safety. As it happened, however, Hsieh Fu of K'uai-chi suddenly died. The people of K'uai-chi consequently laughed at the people of Wu, saying, "Your man tried to make it, but ours was the one who was called!"[2]

1. Four stars in the constellation Leo; according to Chinese belief, they correspond in the world of the heavens to the lesser officials and recluses of the terrestrial world.

2. Hsieh Fu's death was interpreted as proof that Heaven had recognized him as superor in virtue to Tai K'uei. The final sentence is translated somewhat freely in order to bring out the meaning.

53

阮宣杖頭
JUAN HSÜAN – at the tip of his staff

畢卓甕下
PI CHO – beside the wine jars

According to the *History of the Chin*, Juan Hsiu, whose polite name was Hsüan-tzu, was a cousin of the high official Juan Hsien. He had a great fondness for the *Book of Changes* and the writings of Lao Tzu, and was skilled at the kind of philosophical discussion known as "pure conversation." Simple and easy-going by nature, he paid no attention to the affairs of the world. Whenever he went out walking, he would tie a packet of a hundred cash to the tip of his walking stick, and when he came to a wine shop, he would immediately go in and get merrily drunk by himself. No matter how rich or eminent the men of the time, he never deigned to give them so much as a glance. His house was often without a peck or parcel of provisions, yet he remained utterly unconcerned. He was always to be found in the company of his relatives or like-minded friends, enjoying himself among the woods and hills. Wang Yen engaged him in discussions on the *Book of Changes*, and though he used few words, his ideas were so penetrating that Wang Yen could only sigh with admiration.

Juan Hsiu continued to live in poverty until he was over forty, and as a result had never taken a wife. Wang Tun and others presented him with gifts of money, urging him to become their son-in-law. All the most famous men of the time, struck by his personality, pressed their contributions upon him, but he refused to heed their offers. Later he became equerry to the heir apparent. In the time of troubles [A.D. 317] he fled from the capital, but was killed by brigands.

Pi Cho of the Chin, whose polite name was Mou-shih, was a native of T'ung-yang in Hsin-ts'ai.

From his youth he showed a penchant for free and unconventional behavior. He became an official in the board of civil office, but constantly drank wine and neglected his duties. One of his neighbor officials brewed some wine and it had just reached the stage for drinking. Pi Cho, emboldened by what he had already drunk, stole in at night among the neighbor's wine jars and began to help himself. The watchman in charge of the wine caught him at it and tied him up. When morning came and the watchman discovered that the culprit was none other than Pi Cho of the board of civil office, he hurriedly untied the bonds. Pi Cho, however, proceeded to invite the owner of the wine to join him in a party among the wine jars, and got thoroughly drunk before taking his leave.

Pi Cho always used to say to people, "If I could get a boat and fill it with a couple of hundred gallons of wine, and load the stem and stern with the tastiest foods of the four seasons, then with a wine cup in my right hand and a crab's claw in my left, I'd be quite content to spend the rest of my life paddling and floating around in the wine!"

After the Chin dynasty moved its capital south of the Yangtze [A.D. 317], he became a chief clerk under Wen Ch'iao.

54

滕公佳城

LORD T'ENG and the firm fortress

王果石崖

WANG KUO and the rocky cliff

According to the *Hsi-ching tsa-chi* or *Miscellaneous Notes on the Western Capital*, Lord T'eng was once riding in a carriage, about to go out of Ch'ang-an by the Gate to the Eastern Capital, when his horses began to neigh and crouch down. They refused to go any further, but pawed at the ground with their hoofs for a long time. Lord T'eng ordered some of his soldies to dig up the ground where the horses had been pawing, and after they had dug down three feet, they came upon a stone coffin. Lord T'eng examined it by the light of the lamp and discovered that it had an inscription on it. He washed the inscription with water and copied it out, but it was written entirely in peculiar ancient characters and none of his attendants could make out the meaning.

He then consulted the scholar Shu-sun T'ung, who replied, "These are what is known as 'tadpole characters.' " He transcribed the inscription into modern characters, and it read: "Dark, dark, the firm fortress:[1] after three thousand years it shall see the bright sun. Harken! Lord T'eng shall dwell in this chamber." Lord T'eng exclaimed, "Ah, it is fate! When I die, lay me to rest here." When he died, he was accordingly buried in the stone coffin.

Lord T'eng was a man of the Former Han named Hsia-hou Ying, who advanced to the post of master of carriage. He was serving as magistrate of T'eng when he first joined the forces of Kao-tsu, the founder of the Han, acting as his carriage driver, and hence he came to be called Lord T'eng.

According to the *Shen-kuai-chih* or *Record of Supernatural Wonders*, General Wang Kuo was appointed governor of Yi Province. Traveling through the Three Gorges of the Yangtze on the way to his new post, he gazed at the banks of the river from the boat in which he was riding and, where the rocky scarps rose a thousand feet in the air, spied something hanging halfway down the cliff that looked like a coffin. He questioned people who had passed that

127

way before, and they all told him that it had been there for a long time. He then ordered a man to be lowered from the top of the cliff to examine it, and it was found to be indeed a coffin. The bones of the deceased were still in it, and there was a stone with an inscription that read: "After three hundred years the waters will float me and I shall approach the brink of the long Yangtze. I shall hang down, about to fall, about to fall but never falling, and there I shall meet Wang Kuo!"

When Wang Kuo saw the inscription, he was moved to sadness and said, "Several hundred years ago he already knew my name. How could I bear to cast him aside!" He thereupon delayed his journey, conducting burial rites, interring the coffin, and offering sacrifices before proceeding on his way.[2]

1. A term for a coffin. This, and the inscription in the episode that follows, are rhymed in the original.
2. Wang Kuo is known from other sources to have been an official of the early T'ang. This is a rare example of an episode dealing with events of the same period as that of the writer of the *Meng Ch'iu*. Nothing is known of the text called the *Shen-kuai-chih*.

55

馬后大練
EMPRESS MA in coarse-woven silk

孟光荊釵
MENG KUANG with thornwood hairpins

Empress Ma of the Later Han, whose posthumous name was
Ming-te or Bright Virtue, was the youngest daughter of Ma Yüan,
the General Who Calms the Waves. By the age of ten she was
already able to direct household affairs with the competence of an
adult. Once, when she had been suffering from a long illness, her
mother employed a diviner to divine her fate by means of the
milfoil stalks. The diviner replied, "Though this girl has been ill
for a long time, she will later become highly honored. The omens
are such that I can hardly describe them!" Later the mother called
in a physiognomist to examine her daughters and see what fate
lay in store for them. When he examined the future empress, he
said in astonishment. "The time will surely come when I will
acknowledge myself a subject of this girl!"

In time she was chosen to enter the women's quarters of the
palace, and when Emperor Ming came to the throne [A.D. 58], she
was given the rank of Noble Lady. At this time Lady Chia bore
the emperor a son, the future Emperor Chang. Emperor Ming
instructed the future Empress Ma to raise the child, adding, "I
only hope that you will not fail to show the child affection
although he is not your own son." On the contrary, however, she
took even greater pains in raising him than if he had been a child
of her own. The boy in turn proved to be intensely filial in nature,
endowed by Heaven with a sense of kindness and gratitude. The
love and affection that existed between adopted mother and son
showed not the smallest trace of discord.

The authorities presented a memorial to the throne asking that
Lady Ma be established in the Long Autumn Palace [i.e., declared
empress]. The emperor had not yet expressed his opinion in the
matter when his mother, Empress Dowager Yin, exclaimed,
"Lady Ma is the crowning virtue of the women's quarters. She is
the very person to be made empress!" In time Lady Ma was
accordingly set up as empress. After assuming the place of honor

in the inner palace, she conducted herself with even greater modesty and circumspection than before. She was thoroughly versed in the *Book of Changes*, loved to read the *Spring and Autumn Annals* and the *Elegies of Ch'u*, and was particularly fond of the *Rites of Chou* and the works of the Confucian philosopher Tung Chung-shu. She always wore simple robes of coarse-woven silk with no decorative border at the hem.

Liang Hung of the Later Han, whose polite name was Po-luan, was a native of P'ing-ling in Fu-feng.

In the same district there was a family named Meng who had a daughter who was fat, ugly, and dark-complexioned, and so strong she could lift a stone mortar. Having turned down what offers of marriage came her way until she had reached the age of thirty, she was asked by her mother and father to explain her reasons. "I want someone of true worth like Po-luan!" she replied. Liang Hung, hearing of this, made arrangements to marry her.

When she first entered the gate of her new home as a bride, she wore her best clothes and adornments. But seven days passed and her husband disdained even to speak to her. She asked what fault she had committed, whereupon Liang Hung replied, "I wanted a woman dressed in leather and felt, one who could join me in living the life of a recluse deep in the mountains. But here you are robed in fancy silks and daubed with paint and powder. This isn't what I was looking for at all!"

"I have clothes for living the country life!" said his wife, and presently she reappeared with her hair done up in a simple mallet-shaped hairdo and wearing a hemp robe, tending to her household chores where her husband could see her. Liang Hung was overjoyed and exclaimed, "This is the real wife for Liang Hung!" Although her name was Meng Kuang, he always addressed her by her polite name Te-yüeh as a sign of respect. Eventually they went off together to live in the mountains of Pa-ling.[1]

---

1. The "thornwood hairpins" mentioned in the *Meng Ch'iu* couplet derive from the biography of Meng Kuang in Huang-fu Mi's *Lieh-nü-chuan*, which records that she customarily wore "thornwood hairpins and hemp skirts." Liang Hung and Meng Kuang have become symbolic in Chinese literature of the perfectly matched couple.

56

巫 馬 戴 星
Wu-MA walks by starlight

宓 賤 彈 琴
Fu CHIEN strums the lute

The *Lü-shih ch'un-ch'iu* or *Spring and Autumn of Mr. Lü* records that when Fu Tzu-chien governed the region of Shan-fu, he spent his time strumming a lute and never stepped out of his office, and yet Shan-fu was well governed. When Wu-ma Ch'i held the same post, he would set off by starlight and come home by starlight, day and night without rest, tending to everything in person – and Shan-fu was once more well governed.

Wu-ma Ch'i asked Fu Tzu-chien the reason for this seeming anomaly. Fu Tzu-chien replied, "One might say that I trust to others, while you trust to your own efforts. Those who trust to their own efforts are bound to have a hard time of it; those who trust to others are bound to have it easy."[1]

1. Both men are mentioned in the *Analects* and have traditionally been regarded as disciples of Confucius.

57

郝 廉 留 錢
Ho LIEN leaves a coin

雷 義 送 金
LEI YI rejects the gold

According to the *Feng-su-t'ung* or *Survey of Manners and Customs*, Ho Tzu-lien could never get enough food to satisfy his hunger or enough clothes to fend off the cold, yet he refused to accept a particle of assistance from others. Once he visited his elder sister and was invited to a meal, but he left a coin under his cushion before departing. And whenever he was away from home and was given a drink of water, he would always throw a coin down the well by way of payment.

Lei Yi of the Later Han, whose polite name was Chung-kung, was a native of P'o-yang in Yü-chang.

He began his career as a clerk in charge of documents in the provincial office, where he helped to recommend and promote men of worth, but never boasted of what he had done. Once he succeeded in saving the life of a man who had been condemned to death for some offense. The man subsequently presented him with two catties of gold as an expression of gratitude, but Lei Yi refused to accept the gift. The owner of the gold then watched for an opportunity when Lei Yi was not at home and, without telling anyone, threw the gold up on top of the rafter of the house. Later, when the roof was being repaired, the gold came to light. By this time the owner of the gold was dead and it was impossible to return it to him, so Lei Yi turned it over to the district officials.

In time he was chosen to act as aide to the imperial secretary, and was later appointed magistrate of Nan-tun.

58

王喬雙鳬

WANG CH'IAO – a pair of mallards

華佗五禽

HUA T'O – the five creatures

Wang Ch'iao of the Later Han was a native of Ho-tung who was appointed magistrate of the district of She. He possessed supernatural arts, and on the first and fifteenth days of each month would invariably appear at court to pay his respects. Emperor Ming [A.D. 58–75], puzzled that he came to the capital so often but never seemed to have any carriage or horse, secretly ordered the grand historian to observe his arrival from a distance. The grand historian reported that whenever it was time for Wang Ch'iao to appear, a pair of mallards would invariably be seen winging in from the south. The grand historian thereupon watched for the arrival of the mallards and stretched a bird net to catch them, but all he got in the net was a pair of shoes.

Later Heaven sent down a jade coffin that came to rest in front of the hall of Wang Ch'iao's office. Wang Ch'iao exclaimed, "Is the Emperor of Heaven sending for me alone?" He then bathed, washed his hair, put on his robes and adornments, and lay down in the coffin, whereupon the lid promptly fitted itself into place. He was buried east of the city, and the common people erected a funerary temple in his honor, calling it the Shrine of the Lord of She.

Hua T'o of the Later Han, whose polite name was Yüan-hua, was a native of Ch'iao in the state of P'ei.

He was conversant with a number of classical texts and enlightened in the art of nurturing health. Even when he was close to a hundred years old he retained his youthful appearance, and the people of the time looked on him as an immortal.

He was highly skilled in medicine, though he never prescribed more than a few different varieties of drugs and never applied acupuncture or moxabustion treatment to more than a few spots on the body. If a disease developed within the internal organs, where medicine and acupuncture could not reach it, he would first order the patient to drink "hemp-boil concoction" mixed with wine.[1] After the patient was drunk and could no longer feel anything, he would then cut open the belly or back and excise the mass of affected matter. If the ailment was in the intestine or stomach, he would make an incision in the organ, wash it, and remove the diseased area. After such operations, he would sew up the incision and apply a miraculous ointment. In four or five days the incision would heal, and by the time a month had passed, the patient would be completely recuperated.

Hua T'o was a man of evil disposition, and moreover considered it a disgrace to make a living as a doctor. The military leader Ts'ao Ts'ao [A.D. 155–220], under whom he had earlier served, repeatedly sent letters summoning him, but again and again he failed to appear when he had promised to do so, and in the end Ts'ao Ts'ao had him put to death.

Wu P'u of Kuang-ling studied under Hua T'o, and Hua T'o said to him, "The human body ought to have work and exercise – only one should never carry them to an extreme. With proper exercise, the vitality of the grain one eats can be properly digested, the blood will circulate freely in the veins, and sickness will have no opportunity to develop. Then the body will be like a door hinge that never rots no matter how long it is used. The immortals of ancient times had their breathing and stretching exercises, their bear-hangings and owl-glances, by which they stretched and pulled the hips and body and exercised the various joints, in this way seeking to prevent aging.

"I have a technique of my own which I call the Games of the Five Creatures. The first is called Tiger, the second Deer, the third Bear, the fourth Monkey, and the fifth Bird. They help to get rid of illness and at the same time strengthen the legs and feet, and thus correspond to the breathing and stretching of the ancients. If you feel some discomfort in the body, then stand up and do the games of one of these creatures. You will feel relaxed and the sweat will pour out. Then apply powder, and your whole body will seem to be light and easy and you will have a good appetite." Wu P'u carried out these instructions, and even when he was over ninety years of age his hearing and eyesight remained keen and all of his teeth were sound.

1. Though the Chinese in early times were well aware of the narcotic and medicinal properties of hemp, the word translated here as "hemp" may have some other meaning. For a discussion of the passage, see Needham, Joseph, *Science and Civilisation in China*, Vol. 5, Part 2 (Cambridge Univ. Press, 1974), p. 151, n. d.

59

馮媛當熊
LADY FENG faces a bear

班女辭輦
LADY PAN declines a cart ride

The Bright Companion Lady Feng, concubine of Emperor Yüan [48–33 B.C.] of the Former Han, was the daughter of the general of the right Feng Feng-shih and the grandmother of Emperor P'ing.[1] She was in time honored with the rank of Beautiful Companion and within the palace held a place in the affections of the ruler equal to that of the Bright Companion Fu.

The emperor, accompanied by the women of the palace, once visited the so-called tiger pens to watch the wild animals fight. The group had taken their seats when a bear broke out of the pen, climbed the railing, and was on the point of entering the hall where the emperor and his party were sitting. The Bright Companion Fu and the other ladies in attendance all ran away in terror, but Lady Feng walked straight toward the bear and stood in its way.

After the beast had been killed by guards, the emperor said, "It is only human nature to be terrified in such a situation. What made you walk in the direction of the bear?"

Lady Feng replied, "If a wild beast has a human being to seize upon, it will halt its attack. I was afraid that the bear would advance to where Your Majesty was seated, and therefore I put myself in its way."

Emperor Yüan sighed with admiration and his respect and affection for Lady Feng doubled.

The Beautiful Companion Pan, concubine of Emperor Ch'eng [32–7 B.C.] of the Former Han, was the daughter of the commander of Yüeh cavalry Pan K'uang. Once the emperor was amusing himself in the women's quarters and invited Lady Pan to ride with him in his hand-drawn cart, but she declined, saying, "In the paintings of ancient times one always sees the sage rulers with eminent ministers by their side; only the last rulers of the Three Dynasties, the men who brought destruction to their lines, have their women favorites beside them. Now if you invite me to share your cart, will you not appear to resemble the latter?"

The emperor, impressed with her words, abandoned the idea. When his mother the empress dowager heard of the incident, she was pleased and said, "In ancient times it was Lady Fan, nowadays it's the Beautiful Companion Pan!"[2]

Later Chao Fei-yen, another of the emperor's concubines, slanderously accused Empress Hsü and Lady Pan of resorting to sorcery to win favor, attempting to put a curse on the other women of the palace, and extending their imprecations even to the person of the ruler. When Lady Pan was cross-examined by the law officials, she replied, "I have heard that life and death are decreed by fate, and wealth and eminence are decided by Heaven.[3] Even when one follows correct behavior he cannot be certain of good fortune, so what could he hope for by committing evil? If the gods have understanding, then they will not listen to the pleas of a disloyal subject; and if they have no understanding, what good would it do to offer pleas to them? Therefore I would never resort to such actions!"

The emperor, impressed with her answer, took pity on her and awarded her a gift of a hundred catties of gold.

1. The text erroneously reads "general of the left;" I have followed the reading in *Han shu* 97B.
2. Because the king of Ch'u in ancient times was excessively fond of hunting, his concubine Lady Fan refused to eat meat as a form of protest. Lady Pan has shown herself to be a similar model of behavior in correcting the faults of her lord.
3. Lady Pan is quoting from *Analects* XII, 5.

60

王 充 閲 市

WANG CH'UNG reads in the marketplace

董 生 下 帷

MASTER TUNG lowers the curtains

Wang Ch'ung of the Later Han, whose polite name was Chung-jen, was a native of Shang-yü in K'uai-chi.

His family was poor and he had no books. When he was a student at the state university in Lo-yang, he always used to wander among the stalls in the marketplace of the capital, reading the books that were put out for sale. One look at a book and he would immediately be able to recite it from memory, and thus in the end he became widely learned in a number of different subjects and familiar with the words of all the hundred schools of philosophy.

He entered government service, holding the post of clerk in charge of documents in the provincial office. He was very fond of discussions and theories, and though his ideas often at first seemed quite perverse and outlandish, in the end they would be found to conform to reason and reality. He believed that the common run of Confucian scholars stuck too closely to the letter of the text and often missed the true meaning. He thereupon shut his door and immersed himself in thought, absenting himself from all the ordinary ceremonies of social life. He ranged the walls and windowsills with writing brushes and scrapers and in time produced a work in eighty-five sections entitled *Lun heng* or *Critical Essays*, in which he expounded on the similarities and differences among various categories of things and rectified the errors and confusions that existed in the customs of the times.[1]

The provincial director selected him to act as one of his assistants, and later promoted him to the post of sub-director, but Wang Ch'ung in time submitted his resignation and returned to his home. Though Emperor Chang [A.D. 76–88] sent a government carriage to his home with a summons to return to official service, he declined to do so.

Tung Chung-shu of the Former Han was a native of Kuang-

138

ch'uan. In his youth he studied the *Spring and Autumn Annals*, and in the reign of Emperor Ching [156–141 B.C.] was made an erudite. He used to lower the curtains of his room when he lectured in order to avoid distraction. His older disciples would pass on what they had learned to the newer ones, so that some of his students had never seen his face. Three years he taught in this way and never once took the time even to look out into his garden; such was his devotion to his task. In all his activities he never did anything that was not in accord with ritually prescribed behavior, and all the other scholars looked up to him as their teacher.

He was recommended to Emperor Wu [140–87 B.C.] as a man of worth and goodness and replied to the questions put on the civil service examination, after which he was appointed to the post of prime minister of the state of Chiang-tu. There he served under King Yi, the ruler of the state, who was an elder brother of Emperor Wu and a man arrogant in nature and fond of daring. Tung Chung-shu, however, succeeded in correcting the king's faults through the principles of ritual and rectitude, and the king in turn respected him highly.

In managing affairs of state,[2] Tung Chung-shu studied the various natural disasters and portentous happenings recorded in the *Spring and Autumn Annals* and on the basis of this study attempted to discover the principles behind the operations and interactions of the yin and yang. He concluded that if one wished rain to fall, one should shut off the yang forces and free those of the yin, while if one wished the rain to cease, one should do the reverse. By applying these methods he never failed to achieve the desired effect.

Kung-sun Hung also studied the *Spring and Autumn Annals*, but was no match for Tung Chung-shu. However, by following the trend of the times and supporting the undertakings of the emperor, he succeeded in reaching the position of a high minister in the government. Tung Chung-shu regarded him as no more than a servile flatterer. Kung-sun Hung for this reason hated Tung Chung-shu and advised the emperor to appoint him as prime minister to the king of Chiao-hsi. The king of Chiao-hsi was also an elder brother of the emperor. He was extremely willful and unruly, but he had heard of Tung Chung-shu's reputation as a great Confucian scholar and, contrary to Kung-sun Hung's hopes, treated him very well. Thus Tung Chung-shu served as prime minister under two strong-minded lords, but by behaving correctly himself and guiding those under him, submitting reprimands to the ruler from time to time, and spreading the teachings of Confucianism throughout the state, he was able to bring about good order wherever he was.

After leaving government service, he gave no thought to accumulating wealth for his family but devoted himself entirely to studying and writing books. Whenever some important ceremony was to be held at court, a messenger was dispatched to consult his opinion, and his advice at such times was in all cases reasonable and in accordance with correct practice.

From the time when Tou Ying and T'ien Fen in turn served as chancellor [140–131 B.C.], Confucianism flourished. Tung Chung-shu in his answers to the examination questions urged the government to spread the teachings of Confucius and to take steps to discourage the other doctrines of the hundred schools of philosophy. The establishment of the state university staffed with official teachers, and the custom of calling on the various provinces to recommend young men of outstanding talent and filial conduct and integrity to attend it, both came about as a result of Tung Chung-shu's proposals. He died in his home of old age. His family later moved to Mou-ling and his sons and grandsons all advanced to high office

1. At this time writing was often done on strips of wood. If one made a mistake, one could correct it by scraping the surface clean with a scraper.
2. The Han period "kings" were not permitted to govern, all such matters being handled by the prime minister and other officials appointed by and responsible to the imperial court.

61

宿瘤採桑

OLD WEN picks mulberry leaves

漆室憂葵

LACQUER ROOM worries about her mallows

According to the old *Lieh-nü-chuan* or *Biographies of Outstanding Women*, the consort of King Min [323–284 B.C.] of Ch'i had a large wen on her neck and was called Old Wen. When the king was young, he once went on an outing, traveling as far as the eastern sector of the outer wall of the capital. All the common people turned out to watch, but Old Wen, then a young girl, went right on picking mulberry leaves as before.[1] The king, puzzled by such behavior, questioned her, saying, "Whenever I leave the palace on an outing, the common people, young and old alike, all come to watch. Why do you alone not give me so much as a glance?"

She replied, "I was told by my father and mother to pick mulberry leaves. I was not told to watch Your Majesty!"

"This is an unusual young woman!" said the king. "Too bad she has that wen on her neck."

But the young woman said, "It is not the business of a humble girl like myself to attend to two tasks at once. As long as I don't forget what I've been told to do, what is the complaint? What harm does a wen do?"

The king, much pleased, exclaimed, "This is a wise young woman!" and ordered that she be placed in one of the carriages in his train.

But the girl said, "I have a father and mother at home. If I were to go off with Your Majesty without having received instructions from them to do so, I would be a wayward daughter. What use would you have for such a person?"

The king, much ashamed of himself, allowed her to go home, but later he dispatched messengers to go to her house with betrothal gifts in accordance with the proper ritual, as well as a sum of a hundred taels of gold, and present them to her family. Her father and mother, overwhelmed with confusion, urged her to bathe, wash her hair, and put on some other clothes, but she said,

"This is the way the king saw me. If I put on other clothing and change my appearance, he won't recognize me!" Accordingly she went off to the palace with the king's messengers dressed just as she was.

After King Min had made her his consort, she gave orders to decrease the size of the women's quarters of the palace, fill in the pleasure ponds, cut down the portions of food, and perform music less frequently, and forbade the women of the palace to wear robes of more than one color. By the end of a year, her good influence had extended even to neighboring states, and their rulers came to pay respects at the court of Ch'i. The king's forces invaded the smaller states of Han, Wei, and Chao, and even inspired terror in the great states of Ch'in and Ch'u. All of this was due to the efforts of Old Wen. After she died, however, the state of Yen invaded Ch'i, massacring its people, and King Min was forced to flee abroad, where he was assassinated.

According to the old *Lieh-nü-chuan* or *Biographies of Outstanding Women*, there was a young woman of the village of Lacquer Room in the state of Lu who, though past the usual age, had not yet found a husband. Lu was at this time under the rule of Duke Mu [409–377 B.C.], an old man whose heir was still a child. The young woman of Lacquer Room leaned against a pillar of her house and sighed. "Why these sad sighs?" asked the woman next door. "Is it because you want to get married?"

"Why would I be sad just because I'm not married?" said the young woman. "I'm worried because the ruler of Lu is an old man and his heir still a child."

The woman next door laughed and said, "That's something for the grandees of Lu to worry about. What does it have to do with us women?"

"That's not so!" said the young woman. "Once in the past a visitor from the state of Chin put up at my house and tied his horse to a tree in the garden. But the horse broke loose and trampled all over my mallows, and as a result I had to go a whole year without eating mallow greens. Another time, some girl in the neighborhood ran off with a man, and her family hired my elder brother to chase after them. But he ran into torrential rains and was drowned in the flood, and as a result I have to go through life without my elder brother. They say that the Yellow River spreads its moisture for nine miles along its bank and innundates the area for three hundred paces around. If the state of Lu has troubles, then ruler and subject, father and son will all have to bear the shame, and misfortune will spread to the whole population. How could we women alone escape its effects!"

Three years later, Lu was in fact torn by internal dissension. Ch'i and Ch'u took the opportunity to launch attacks on it, and there were repeated outbreaks of banditry. The men went off to fight, and the women worked at transporting supplies and had no time for a moment's rest.

1. To feed to silkworms.

62

阮 簡 曠 達

JUAN CHIEN takes the broad view

袁 耽 俊 邁

YÜAN KENG truly excels

The old commentary, quoting from the *Discussion of the Seven Worthies of the Bamboo Grove*, records that Juan Chien, a nephew of Juan Hsien, was also, like Hsien, a man of broad and liberal views who did very much as he pleased. While in mourning for his father, he once went on a trip and ran into a heavy snowstorm and severe cold. Eventually he stopped at the official residence of the magistrate of Ling-i. The magistrate had had a meal of boiled millet and meat broth prepared for some other guests,[1] but Juan Chien helped himself to the food and ended up engaging in philosophical discussion. As a result he was ignored and shunned by the world for almost twenty years.

Yüan Keng of the Chin, whose polite name was Yen-tao, was a native of Yang-hsia in Ch'en Province. From his youth he displayed great talent, outshining the common run of men and refusing to bow to convention, and was praised by the gentlemen of the time.

When the powerful statesman and military leader Huan Wen was young, he used to amuse himself gambling. He exhausted all his family's wealth, but still found himself with gambling debts. He tried to think of some way to pay them but could hit on no solution, and so he determined to go to Yüan Keng for help. Yüan Keng was in mourning for one of his parents at the time, but Huan Wen decided to try telling him his troubles anyway. Yüan Keng showed no particular sign of objection, and in the end changed out of his mourning clothes, stuffed his hemp mourning cap into the breast of his robe, and went along with Huan Wen to the creditor's house for a game of *liu-po*.[2]

Yüan Keng had long been famous for his skill at the game, and the creditor had in fact heard of his reputation but did not know him by sight. "I don't expect you can play as well as Yüan Keng," the creditor remarked before they began. Once they had seated

144

themselves at the board, Yüan Keng was in no time betting a hundred thousand cash on one play, and eventually ran his winnings up to the sum of a million cash. He then threw down the dice, gave a loud shout, and, pulling the hemp mourning cap out of his robe and flinging it on the floor, said, "*Now* do you know who Yüan Keng is?" This is the kind of liberal-minded and unconventional man he was. In official service he held the post of gentleman in assistance.

1. "Millet and meat broth" follows the version of the anecdote quoted in Liu Hsiao-piao's commentary on *Shih-shuo hsin-yü* sec. 23. All of Juan Hsien's actions are, of course, contrary to the spirit and letter of traditional mourning customs.
2. A game like backgammon played with dice and pieces on a board. Yüan Keng lived in the early years of the 4th century.

63

Su Wu holds on to the credentials

鄭 衆 不 拜

CHENG CHUNG refuses to kowtow

Su Wu of the Former Han, whose polite name was Tzu-ch'ing, was a native of Tu-ling.

In the time of Emperor Wu [140–87 B.C.] he was appointed general of palace attendants, given the imperial credentials, and dispatched as envoy to the Hsiung-nu. The *Shan-yü*, the chief of the Hsiung-nu tribes, hoping to force Su Wu to surrender and acknowledge allegiance, had him confined to a large storage pit and deprived of all food and drink. But there was a snowfall and Su Wu, lying on the floor of the pit, chewed up the felt of his garments along with the snow and managed to swallow it down, so that several days passed and he remained alive. The Hsiung-nu thereupon concluded that he must be a god. Eventually he was moved to an uninhabited region along the shores of the Northern Sea [Lake Baikal], where he was set to herding rams. "When your rams give milk, you may return!" he was told. The rod identifying him as an imperial envoy he used for a staff when he herded his sheep, asleep or awake holding tight to it, until the hairs of the yak tail that decorated the tip had all dropped out.

After Emperor Chao came to the throne [86 B.C.], the Hsiung-nu established peaceful relations with the Han. The Han asked for the return of Su Wu and the others of his party, but the Hsiung-nu lied and reported that Su Wu was dead. When an envoy from the Han journeyed to the territory of the Hsiung-nu, Ch'ang Hui, a member of Su Wu's original party, instructed him to say, "The Son of Heaven, hunting in his Shang-li Park, shot down a wild goose, and tied to its leg was a letter written on silk which said that Su Wu and the others were to be found in such-and-such swamp!"[1] As a result, Su Wu was able to return to China.

He was appointed director of dependent states, a post drawing the salary of a full two-thousand-picul official, and was presented with two million in cash, two *ch'ing* of public lands, and a house and grounds. Su Wu had remained among the Hsiung-nu for nineteen years. When he first set out, he was a vigorous man in the prime of life, but by the time he returned, his hair and beard had turned completely white. During the reign of Emperor Hsüan [73–49 B.C.], because he was an elderly official renowned for his integrity, he was allowed to attend court on the first and fifteenth days of the month and was awarded the title of sacrificer of wine. He was over eighty when he died. Later, he was included among the group of eminent men whose portraits were painted in the Unicorn Hall. A likeness was made of each man, identified with his office, fief, family name and personal name.

Cheng Chung of the Later Han, whose polite name was Chung-shih, was a native of K'ai-feng in Ho-nan. He applied himself diligently to scholarship and soon made a name for himself in the world.

At the beginning of the *yung-p'ing* era [A.D. 58–75] he was recognized as an "expert in the Classics" and was made a steward of the palace. In the eighth year of the same era he was given the imperial credentials and dispatched as envoy to the Hsiung-nu. When he reached the Northern Court, as the headquarters of the Hsiung-nu was called, he found that the wretches wanted him to kowtow to the *Shan-yü*. Cheng Chung, however, refused to stoop to such a humiliating demand. The *Shan-yü*, greatly angered, had him placed under strict confinement and deprived of all water and fire, hoping to force him to submit. Cheng Chung then drew his sword and vowed to take his own life, whereupon the *Shan-yü*, fearful of the consequences, gave up his efforts and allowed Cheng Chung to return to China.

Later the emperor wanted to send Cheng Chung once more to the Hsiung-nu. Cheng Chung said, "When I formerly carried out the imperial command to act as envoy, I refused to kowtow to the Hsiung-nu, and the *Shan-yü*, enraged, sent his soldiers to surround me and hold me in confinement. If now I am once more ordered to face the Hsiung-nu, I am certain to be subjected to insult and intimidation. In truth I cannot bear to go with the credentials of the Great Han and kowtow in the presence of those barbarians in their felts and skins!" The emperor, however, refused to heed his request and Cheng Chung was obliged to set off on his journey. Along the way he continued to send letters to the court strongly urging that the mission be canceled. The emperor finally sent orders that he be brought back and handed over in chains to the commandant of justice. Because of an amnesty, he was in time allowed to return to his home.

Later, when the emperor received envoys from the Hsiung-nu, he asked them about the struggle that had gone on between Cheng Chung and the *Shan-yü* over the question of etiquette, and they all replied that Cheng Chung had displayed a firmness and daring that could not have been surpassed by Su Wu himself. The emperor summoned him to official service once more, appointing him a marshal of the army. He held the post of minister of agriculture at the time of his death.

1. Because of this incident, the *yen* or wild goose has come to be a standard symbol in Chinese literature for letters.

64

郭巨將坑
KUO CHÜ prepares a pit

董永自賣
TUNG YUNG sells himself

The old commentary, quoting from the *Hsiao-tzu-chuan* or *Biographies of Filial Sons*, records that Kuo Chü of the Later Han was a poor man who took good care of his aged mother. His wife gave birth to a son, and when the child was two and had been weaned,[1] the old woman began to eat less, always giving the remainder to her grandson.

Kuo Chü said to his wife, "We are too poor to provide food for so many. You and I must go together and bury the child in a pit. We can always have more children, but I can never get another mother!" His wife did not dare oppose his wishes. Kuo Chü accordingly began to dig a pit, but when he had dug down some two feet or more, he suddenly saw a large measuring-pot full of gold. On the pot it said: "Heaven presents this to the filial son Kuo Chü. No official can seize it, no man can take it away!"

According to the old commentary, Tung Yung of the Han, having lost his mother at an early age, was left with the care of his father. His family was poor and he was obliged to work as a hired laborer in the fields. When the farming season came around, he would put his father in a small cart and push him to the fields. There he would seat the old man in the shade beneath a tree by the side of the fields while he went about his farm labors. When his father died, he went to his employer and asked to borrow ten thousand cash, promising to sell himself into slavery in return; in this way he was finally able to secure the money needed for his father's funeral.

As he was returning home from the funeral, he suddenly met a young woman along the road who was very beautiful in face and figure. The woman asked to become Tung Yung's wife. Tung Yung went with her to see his employer, who agreed that if the woman would weave three hundred bolts of fine silk for him, he would set both husband and wife free. She thereupon applied herself to the weaving and in one month completed the task. The employer was baffled at such rapidity but in the end set the couple free. When they left the employer's house and reached the spot on the road where they had first met, the wife took leave of Tung Yung, saying, "I am the Weaving Maiden of Heaven.[2] Because of your extreme filial piety, the Emperor of Heaven commanded me to help you in repaying your debt." When she had finished speaking, she soared up into the sky and disappeared.

1. Three years old by Chinese reckoning, since a child is regarded as one year old at its birth.
2. A constellation that includes the star Vega.

65

伯道無兒
TENG YU without a son

秬紹不孤
HSI SHAO not an orphan

According to the *History of the Chin*, Teng Yu, whose polite name was Po-tao, was a native of Hsiang-ling in P'ing-yang.

While he was serving as governor of Ho-tung, he was taken prisoner by the rebel leader Shih Le. Eventually he smashed his carriage and, placing his wife and family on a horse and ox, managed to flee. Once more he encountered bandits, however, who seized his horse and ox, and Teng Yu and his wife had to hurry along on foot, carrying on their shoulders Teng Yu's own son and Sui, the son of his younger brother. Teng Yu, perceiving that he could not save both children, finally said to his wife, "My younger brother died early and left only this one son. It is my duty to see that his line does not die out. The only thing to do is to abandon our own son. If we are fortunate enough to escape alive, we will surely be able to have another son." His wife, weeping, consented to do as he wished and they accordingly abandoned their own son. But although they abandoned the boy in the morning, by evening he had caught up with them again, and so the following morning they bound him to a tree and left him.

In time Teng Yu and his wife made their way to the area south of the Yangtze, where the Chin dynasty had established a new court after fleeing from the north [A.D. 317], and Teng Yu was appointed right archery captain in the office of palace writers. His wife, however, never again became pregnant. After settling in the south, Teng Yu accordingly took a concubine whom he treated with great affection. When he inquired about her family, she replied that she had been born in the north but had fled in the time of troubles. She could still remember the family and personal names of her father and mother, and through this Teng Yu discovered that she was his own niece, the child of one of his sisters. Teng Yu had always been a man of virtuous ways, and when he learned this, he was filled with horror and never again took a concubine. Thus he died without an heir.

151

The people of the time, admiring his righteousness and moved to pity by his fate, used to say, "Is the way of Heaven so unknowing that it causes Teng Yu to be without a son?" When Teng Yu died, his brother's son Sui carried out the three-year mourning for him.

Hsi Shao of the Chin, whose polite name was Yen-tsu, was the son of the poet-official Hsi K'ang. Hsi K'ang was very friendly with Shan T'ao, and when he was about to be put to death on charges of improper behavior, he said to his son, "As long as Shan T'ao is alive you will not be an orphan."

Later Shan T'ao recommended Hsi Shao and he was appointed assistant to the private secretary. When Hsi Shao first came to the capital at Lo-yang, someone remarked to Wang Jung, "Yesterday I saw Hsi Shao for the first time among a crowd of people. He stood out as clearly as a wild crane among a flock of chickens!" P'ei Wei also was deeply impressed by him and used to say, "If we had Hsi Shao acting as head of the board of civil affairs, we could be certain that there would be no men of talent anywhere in the empire who were overlooked!"

Hsi Shao continued to advance in office until he held the post of attendant in the inner palace. When Emperor Hui was forced by revolt to leave the capital [A.D. 304], Hsi Shao hastened to the emperor's temporary headquarters. The imperial forces suffered defeat at the hands of the rebels and the various officials and guards fled or were cut down. Hsi Shao alone, awesome in his court robes and hat, in person guarded and protected the emperor. The fighting reached the very area where the emperor sat in his hand-drawn carriage and showers of arrows rained down on the spot. In the end Hsi Shao died by the side of the emperor, his blood spattering the imperial robes. The emperor was deeply grieved and, after the revolt had been put down and the emperor's attendants wished to wash the soiled robes, the emperor said, "This is the blood of the palace attendant Hsi. Do not remove it!"

Later, Emperor Yüan as a mark of honor conferred upon Hsi Shao the post of grand commandant and the posthumous title Chung-mu or "Loyal and Reverent," and offered a *t'ai-lao* sacrifice to his spirit.[1]

1. The most elaborate type of sacrifice, in which an ox, a sheep, and a pig are offered.

66

綠珠墜樓

Lu-chu falls from the tower

文君當壚

Wen-chün minds the counter

According to the *History of the Chin*, Shih Ch'ung, whose polite name was Chi-lun, was a native of Nan-p'i in Po-hai, and was appointed to the post of colonel of the guard.

He had a singing girl called Lu-chu or Green Pearl who was very beautiful, charming, and skilled at playing the flute. The chief of palace writers Sun Hsiu sent a messenger to Shih Ch'ung's house to ask for her. Shih Ch'ung was at the time at his country estate in Chin-ku seated on a cool terrace overlooking the clear streams with his women attendants about him. When the messenger explained his mission, Shih Ch'ung brought out all his maids and concubines and showed them to him, some twenty or thirty women, all scented with orchid and musk and dressed in fine silks and gauzes, and said, "Pick out the one you want!"

"I was ordered to bring back Lu-chu," the messenger explained, "but I don't know which one she is."

Shih Ch'ung was incensed and said, "Lu-chu is my favorite! He cannot have her!"

Sun Hsiu, angered at the refusal, thereupon persuaded Ssu-ma Lun, the king of Chao, to arrange to have Shih Ch'ung put to death. The king of Chao, who wielded extraordinary power, accordingly forged an imperial command calling for the arrest of Shih Ch'ung. Shih Ch'ung was feasting in the upper story of a tower in his home when the soldiers came to the gate to arrest him. "It is because of you that I am being condemned to punishment!" he said to Lu-chu.

Weeping, she replied, "It is only right that I should lay down my life in your presence," and with this she threw herself from the tower and fell to her death.

When Shih Ch'ung was taken to the eastern market for execution, he sighed and said, "That wretch intends to help himself to all my wealth and belongings!"

The man who had been ordered to arrest him remarked,

"If you knew that your wealth was going to bring you trouble, why didn't you let go of it sooner?"

Shih Ch'ung had no answer for this, and in the end was put to death [A.D. 300].

Cho Wen-chün of the Former Han was the daughter of Cho Wang-sun, a rich man of Lin-ch'iung in the province of Shu. She was fond of music and had recently been widowed when the young poet Ssu-ma Hsiang-ju came with some other guests to her home. The drinking having reached its height, Ssu-ma Hsiang-ju played the lute, using it to pour out his heart in an effort to win the young girl's attentions. When Ssu-ma Hsiang-ju arrived with his carriage riders, he had displayed a figure of elegant poise and refinement. Wen-chün secretly peered in through the door at him and her heart was filled with delight; she felt an instant love for him, and her only fear was that she could not have him for her husband. That night she ran away with Ssu-ma Hsiang-ju and the two of them galloped off to the city of Ch'eng-tu, where they lived in Hsiang-ju's house, four bare walls with nothing inside. Her father Cho Wang-sun was outraged.

After a while Wen-chün grew unhappy with her new life and said to her husband, "The only thing to do is to go to Lin-ch'iung, borrow some money from my relatives, and find a way to make a living." Accordingly they went to Lin-ch'iung, where they sold their carriage and all their riding equipment and bought a wine-shop. Hsiang-ju left Wen-chün to mind the counter while he himself, dressed in a workman's loincloth, went off on errands with the other hired men or washed the wine vessels at the well in the marketplace.

Cho Wang-sun, hearing how his daughter was living, was filled with shame and, shutting his gates, refused to leave the house. His relatives and the other gentlemen of the town said to him, "You have only one son and two daughters, so you cannot say you lack the funds to help your daughter. It is true that she has ruined her reputation by running off with Ssu-ma Hsiang-ju, but he spent a great deal of time in the past traveling about the country, and though he is poor, he surely has the talent and ability to win success eventually!" In the end Cho Wang-sun gave his daughter a hundred servants and a million cash and she and her husband returned to Ch'eng-tu, where they purchased a house and some fields and lived a life of ease.

Some time after this a man from Shu named Yang Te-i was appointed to serve Emperor Wu [140–87 B.C.] as keeper of the imperial hunting dogs. The emperor happened to come into possession of Ssu-ma Hsiang-ju's poem in rhyme-prose form entitled "Sir Fantasy," which he read with great pleasure. "What a pity that I could not have lived at the same time as the author of this!" said the emperor. Yang Te-i replied, "There is a man named Ssu-ma Hsiang-ju who comes from the same city as I, and he says that he wrote the poem." The emperor was astonished and, summoning Hsiang-ju to the capital, made him a palace attendant.[1]

1. The poem describes the lavish hunts of the feudal lords. After entering imperial service, the poet added a long final section describing the hunts and outings of Emperor Wu. The poem is translated in my *Chinese Rhyme-prose* (New York: Columbia University Press 1971), pp. 29–51.

67

龔遂勸農
Kung Sui encourages agriculture

文翁興學
Wen Weng promotes learning

Kung Sui of the Former Han, whose polite name was Shao-ch'ing, was a native of P'ing-yang in Shan-yang. He was recognized as an "expert in the Classics" and appointed to office.

In the time of Emperor Hsüan [73–49 B.C.], Po-hai and the provinces around it year after year suffered from famine. Thieves and bandits sprang up everywhere and the two-thousand-picul officials were powerless to suppress them. The emperor, after searching about for someone who would be capable of administering wisely, appointed Kung Sui to the post of governor of Po-hai. He was over seventy at the time.

When he reached the border of the province, he sent out letters of instruction to the districts under his jurisdiction ordering them to discharge all the officials who had been appointed to pursue and arrest bandits and thieves. All persons who possessed hoes, sickles, and other farm implements were to be regarded as honest citizens and were not to be subjected to interrogation by the officials; all those who possessed weapons, on the other hand, were to be looked upon as bandits. As a result, the thieves and bandits were completely surpressed and the people were able to live in peace and safety and to take pleasure in their tasks. Kung Sui thereupon opened the granaries and doled out grain to the poor, and endeavored to appoint able officials who would be capable of bringing security to the people and caring for them properly.

Observing that the customs of the old state of Ch'i, in which Po-hai was situated, tended toward luxury and favored secondary occupations over agriculture, he set a personal example by living frugally and encouraging the people to devote themselves to farming and sericulture. He gave orders that each household was to plant one elm tree, a hundred leeks, fifty onions, and one field of scallions, and to raise two sows and five chickens. Those among the people who went about wearing swords and daggers were ordered to sell their swords and buy oxen, and to sell their daggers and buy calves. In time both officials and people came to enjoy affluence and respect and law suits ceased to arise.

Later, Kung Sui was summoned to take office in the capital. His advisory clerk Wang Sheng, who had always been inordinately fond of wine, accompanied him to the capital. As Kung Sui was about to enter the palace, Wang Sheng, who was drunk at the time, said to him, "When the emperor asks you how you were able to restore order to Po-hai, you should reply, 'It was all due to Your Majesty's saintly virtue and not the result of any paltry efforts of mine!' " Kung Sui accordingly replied to the emperor's inquiries in this fashion.

The emperor laughed with delight and said, "How is it that you come to speak in the words of a wise man?"

Kung Sui answered, "I wouldn't have had the wisdom to reply in this fashion, but my advisory clerk instructed me on what to say." The emperor, considering that Kung Sui was too old to be appointed to a high ministerial office, honored him with the post of director of waterworks and appointed Wang Sheng to be his aide, in this way demonstrating his respect and admiration for Kung Sui.[1]

Wen Weng of the Former Han was a native of Shu in Lu-chiang. In his youth he delighted in learning and became an expert in the *Spring and Autumn Annals*.

In the latter part of Emperor Ching's reign [156–141 B.C.], he was appointed governor of the province of Shu.[2] He was a man of kindly disposition and believed in educating the people to virtuous ways. Observing that Shu was a distant border region where barbarian customs prevailed, he set about guiding its people in the direction of progress. He thereupon selected men of talent and perception from among the lesser officials in the provincial and district administrations and personally trained and encouraged them, dispatching them to the capital to receive instruction in the state university from the erudites. After several years these scholars from Shu, having completed their studies, all returned to the region and took up important posts, some of them in time advancing as high as the office of governor or provincial director.

He also established an official school in Ch'eng-tu, the capital of the province, to which he summoned students from the surrounding districts, training them for official position and exempting them from the ordinary duties of corvée labor. Upon completing their studies, those of highest standing were appointed as aides to the provincial and district officials and those of lesser standing were given the rank of filial citizen or diligent worker in the fields.

Whenever Wen Weng went on tours of the districts, he took large numbers of official students who were versed in the Classics and exemplary in conduct along with him, ordering them to spread their teachings abroad and permitting them to come and go in his inner chambers. The officials and people of the province, observing this, were filled with a desire for similar eminence and vied with one another to become government students, men of wealth even putting out sums of money in an effort to obtain the privilege. As a result, the area underwent a major transformation, and students from Shu enjoyed as high a reputation in the capital as those from the old regions of Ch'i and Lu.[3] Emperor Wu thereupon ordered that similar schools be set up in all the provinces and states of the empire; the system of government schools thus originated with Wen Weng.

Wen Weng ended his days in Shu, and after his death, the officials and people established a funerary temple in his honor in which sacrifices were offered at various periods of the year, and continue to be offered today. The fact that even now the regions of Pa and Shu show a fondness for learning and refinement is due to the transforming influence of Wen Weng.

1. The account has been slightly augmented from the biography of Kung Sui in *Han shu* 89.
2. In the region of present-day Szechwan, the western border of China in Han times.
3. The areas in eastern China where Confucianism originated.

68

晏 御 揚 揚
YEN's coachman puffed and proud

五 鹿 嶽 嶽
FIVE DEER's dandy antlers

According to the *Shih chi* or *Records of the Historian*, Yen Ying, whose other names were P'ing and Chung, was prime minister of the state of Ch'i. One day when he went abroad, the wife of his coachman peered out from the gate, observing her husband. As coachman to the prime minister, her husband stationed himself beside the canopy of the big carriage, whipping up his team of four, puffed and proud in spirit and extremely pleased with himself. After he had returned home, his wife asked for permission to leave him.

When he inquired the reason, she replied, "Master Yen is less than six feet in height,[1] yet he holds the position of prime minister of the state of Ch'i and his reputation is honored among all the feudal lords. Observing him as he went abroad, I could see that he is a man of profound forethought and consideration who constantly humbles himself in the presence of others. Now you are eight feet in height, and yet a mere coachman in the service of another man. You, however, make it clear by your attitude that you are quite satisfied with yourself. That is why I have asked for permission to depart!"

After this, her husband took care to conduct himself with greater restraint and humility. Master Yen, puzzled by the transformation, asked him the reason, and he described what had happened. Master Yen thereupon recommended that he be appointed to the rank of grandee.

Wu-lu Ch'ung-tsung of the Former Han, whose polite name was Chün-meng, served as privy treasurer in the time of Emperor Yüan [48–33 B.C.] and enjoyed great favor. He was an expert in the Liang-ch'iu interpretation of the *Book of Changes*.[2] From the time of Emperor Hsüan the Liang-ch'iu school had enjoyed considerable popularity, and Emperor Yüan in particular favored it. Wishing to determine how its interpretations differed from those

160

of other schools, Emperor Yüan commanded Wu-lu Ch'ung-tsung to hold a debate with representatives of the various schools of the *Book of Changes*. Since Wu-lu Ch'ung-tsung enjoyed a position of special favor and was a very eloquent speaker, the other Confucian scholars decided they were no match for him; instead they all pleaded illness, none having courage enough to attend the meeting.

Someone then recommended a scholar named Chu Yün and the emperor had him summoned to the palace. Straightening the hems of his robe, Chu Yün ascended the hall, lifted up his head, and boomed out his challenge in a voice that shook the onlookers. When the two men turned to a debate of difficult points, Chu Yün time and again refuted Master Wu-lu's arguments, and as a result the Confucian scholars made up a saying that went:

> Dandy antlers had Wu-lu [Five Deer]
> But Chu Yü broke them all in two!

Chu Yün was eventually appointed as an erudite.

1. The Chinese foot was about three fourths of an English foot. Yen Tzu or Master Yen, a famous statesman of the Spring and Autumn period, died in 500 B.C.
2. The interpretation of the *I Ching* or *Book of Changes* expounded by Liang-ch'iu Ho, a scholar of the time of Emperor Hsüan (73–49 B.C.).

諸葛顧盧

CHU-KO visited in his hut

69

韓信升壇

HAN HSIN invited to ascend the altar

According to the *Account of Shu,* Chu-ko Liang served as chancellor to Liu Pei, the first ruler of Shu. When Liu Pei fell gravely ill, he summoned Chu-ko Liang to his side and charged him with the conduct of affairs after his death, saying, "You are ten times superior to Ts'ao P'ei.[1] You will surely be able to ensure the safety of the state and complete the great task of unifying the empire. If you find that my heir is worth assisting, then assist him. If he proves to be of no ability, you may take charge yourself!"

Chu-ko Liang, weeping, replied, "I will exert every particle of strength in my limbs to do what duty and loyalty demand and to guard the succession with my life!" Liu Pei also issued an edict to his heir and successor Liu Shan, saying, "You are to conduct affairs in cooperation with the chancellor and serve him as you would a father. From now on all matters, whether great or small, shall be decided by Chu-ko Liang."

On one occasion, Chu-ko Liang submitted a memorial to the ruler, Liu Shan, in which he stated: "I was originally a hemp-robed commoner, farming the fields of Nan-yang. By one means or another I managed to stay alive in those times of chaos, never seeking to win fame among the feudal lords. Your father, the former ruler, did not despise me as a lowly man of no worth, but on the contrary went out of his way to humble himself, three times visiting me in my hut of grass and consulting me on affairs of the time."[2]

In the years of fighting that followed, Chu-ko Liang always used special types of carts known as "wooden oxen" and "streaming horses" to transport food supplies for his army. He made his camp at Wu-chang-yüan in Wu-kung and engaged Ssu-ma Yi of the state of Wei in battle south of the Wei River. The battle continued for over a hundred days, and Chu-ko Liang died in the course of the fighting. He was fifty-four at the time of his death [A.D. 234].

He was given the postumous title Chung-wu or "Loyal and Militant Marquis." He was skilled at calculating the most profitable course of action, and the "rapid-firing crossbows," "wooden oxen," and "streaming horses" which he used were all of his own invention. Basing himself upon texts on the art of war, he devised the Diagrams of the Eight Encampments, each fashioned in such a way as to be highly effective.

Han Hsin of the Former Han was a native of Huai-yin. Since he came from a poor family and had done no outstanding deeds, he was not able to get himself recommended for a position as an official. In time he joined the military leader Hsiang Yü, serving as one of his attendants. He several times offered suggestions on strategy, but Hsiang Yü made no use of them.

He thereupon ran away and joined the forces of Hsiang Yü's rival, the king of Han. The king of Han appointed him to the post of commissary colonel, though he failed to perceive anything unusual about him. Han Hsin several times talked with Hsiao Ho, the king of Han's prime minister, who regarded him with peculiar respect. Han Hsin, deciding that the king of Han had no use for him, once more ran away, but Hsiao Ho went in pursuit of him and after a day or two brought him back. When Hsiao Ho appeared before the king, the latter began to curse him, saying, "Dozens of my generals have deserted me and you did not attempt to pursue a one of them! You must be lying if you tell me you went in pursuit of Han Hsin!"

"Generals are easy enough to get," replied Hsiao Ho, "but a man like Han Hsin has no equal throughout the entire nation. If Your Majesty hopes to contend for mastery of the empire, then Han Hsin is the only man to lay plans with!"

The king thereupon selected an auspicious day, fasted and purified himself, and erected an altar at which he performed a ceremony investing Han Hsin with the rank of major general, much to the astonishment of the entire army. Later Han Hsin was enfeoffed as king of Ch'u and made his capital at Hsia-p'ei. He was accused of plotting revolt but was pardoned and made marquis of Huai-yin. Eventually he was executed by Empress Lü.[3]

1. Ruler of the rival state of Wei; China at this time was divided into the three

contending states of Wei, Shu, and Wu. Chu-ko Liang has appeared earlier in the episode on p. 21.

2. From the famous *Ch'u-shih-piao* or "Memorial on Going to War," submitted to the throne in A.D. 227, in which Chu-ko Liang, preparing to attack the state of Wei, reaffirmed his loyalty to the ruler and offered counsel on affairs of state.

3. King of Han was the title held by Kao-tsu, the founder of the Han dynasty, during his struggle for mastery of the empire; Empress Lü was his consort. Han Hsin was executed in 196 B.C. on suspicion of plotting revolt.

70

王裒柏惨
WANG P'OU – a cypress seared

闵损衣单
MIN SUN – a robe unlined

According to the *History of the Chin*, Wang P'ou, whose polite name was Wei-yüan, was a native of Ying-ling in Ch'eng-yang.

In his youth he determined to become a man of outstanding conduct; he was widely learned and had many talents. His father Wang Yi served as marshal under Emperor Wen but was put to death.[1] Wang P'ou grieved deeply over his father's untimely fate and never sat facing west, the direction of the capital, an indication that he did not acknowledge allegiance to the dynasty. He lived in retirement and gave instruction to students. He built a hut for himself by the grave of his parents and morning and evening invariably used to kneel before the grave mound, grasp the cypress tree that was planted on it, and moan with grief; his tears fell upon the tree until it became seared and withered. His mother had always been frightened of lightning, and after her death, whenever there was a lightning storm, he would immediately hurry to the grave, saying, "I'm right here, mother!"

Whenever he was reading the *Book of Odes* and came to the lines:

Alas, alas, father, mother,
bearing me brought you toil and trail!

he would never fail to read them over several times and weep. As a result, the students receiving instruction from him would always skip over the *Lu-o* poem when they read the text.[2] His family was poor and he worked the fields himself, but he farmed only as many fields and raised only the number of silkworms needed to feed and clothe himself and the members of his household. People offered to assist him, but he declined their offers.

According to the old commentary, Min Sun, whose polite name was Tzu-ch'ien, lost his mother at an early age.[3] His father remarried and had two children by his second wife. Min Sun served his stepmother with the utmost filial piety, never daring to be remiss, but she hated him. She dressed her own children in robes stuffed with floss silk, but Min Sun was obliged to stuff his robe with the fluff from reed flowers.

Once in the depth of winter his father ordered him to drive the carriage for him. Min Sun was so thoroughly chilled in body that he dropped the reins. When his father berated him, he made no attempt to excuse himself, but his father, on looking more closely, discoverd the reason. His father wanted to turn his second wife out of the house, but Min Sun wept and pleaded with him, saying, "While she remains, one child will be cold; but if she leaves, three children will wear unlined robes!" His father, admiring his answer, gave up the idea. His stepmother also had a change of heart and thereafter treated all three children in equal fashion, in the end becoming a model of maternal kindness.

1. Emperor Wen is the posthumous title of Ssu-ma Chao, king of Chin and father of the founder of the Chin dynasty. Wang Yi was executed after suffering defeat in a campaign against the state of Wu in A.D. 252.
2. Mao text #202, the lament of a filial son, in which the lines above appear.
3. Min Tzu-ch'ien is frequently mentioned in the *Analects* as one of the major disciples of Confucius. The source of the present anecdote is uncertain.

71

周公握髮
THE DUKE OF CHOU binds up his hair

蔡邕倒屣
TS'AI YING puts on his sandals backwards

According to the *Shih chi* or *Records of the Historian,* after King
Wu died [traditional date 1116 B.C.], the duke of Chou served as
prime minister to King Wu's son, King Ch'eng. Because the duke
had to remain in the capital, he sent his son Po-ch'in to his fief
in Lu to govern in his place. He admonished his son, saying, "I
am a son of King Wen, a younger brother of King Wu, and uncle
to King Ch'eng. I am thus by no means among the lowly of the
empire. Yet in the course of one hair-washing I bind up my hair
three times, and in the course of one meal I three times spit out
the food in my mouth, always rising in haste to wait upon others,
for I fear that some worthy man of the empire may go overlooked!
When you go to Lu, you must conduct yourself with circumspection and never lord it over others simply because you are the ruler
of a state!"

Ts'ai Ying of the Later Han, whose polite name was Po-chieh,
was a native of Yü in Ch'en-liu.
  In his youth he acquired a broad education, being particularly
fond of literature, mathematics, and astronomy, and he was skilled
in musical performance. He lived a quiet life, practicing the ways
of antiquity and not mingling with the men of the times. Later
he became a general of palace attendants.
  When Emperor Hsien moved the capital west to Ch'ang-an
[A.D. 190], the poet Wang Ts'an also moved to Ch'ang-an.
Ts'ai Ying met him and was deeply impressed. Ts'ai Ying at this
time was famed for his talent and learning and was highly respected at court. Carriages and outriders constantly crowded the
lane where he lived and guests thronged his sitting room. But when
he heard that Wang Ts'an had come to call, he put on his sandals
backwards in his haste to greet him. When Wang Ts'an was led
into the gathering, he proved to be a mere youth of small and
unimposing stature. All the members of the gathering were

startled at Ts'ai Ying's solicitousness, but Ts'ai Ying said, "This is the grandson of great lords and a man of extraordinary talent. I am no match for him. By rights I ought to give him all the books and writings I have in my house!" Wang Ts'an's great-grandfather was Wang Kung and his grandfather was Wang Ch'ang; both were numbered among the three highest ministers of the time.

72

暴 勝 持 斧
PAO SHENG takes his ax in hand

張 綱 埋 輪
CHANG KANG buries his wheels

Pao Sheng-chih of the Former Han went by the polite name
Kung-tzu. In the late years of Emperor Wu's reign [140–87 B.C.]
many thieves and bandits appeared in the provinces and feudal
states. Pao Sheng-chih, acting as a directly appointed envoy of
the emperor, donned embroidered robes, took his ax of authority
in hand, and set out to pursue and seize the criminals, inspecting
the provinces and feudal states east as far as the sea and using
military procedures to punish those who failed to obey the law.
All the surrounding regions trembled at his might.

Chang Kang of the Later Han, whose polite name was Wen-
chi, was a native of Wu-yang in Chien-wei. In his youth he became versed in the Classics and was selected to serve as a clerk in
the censorate.

In the time of Emperor Shun [A.D. 126–44] all affairs of state
were left to the direction of the eunuchs and men of perception
were deeply apprehensive at the situation. Chang Kang too was
filled with constant indignation and said with a sigh, "Filth and
evil crowd the court! Unless I can find some way to volunteer
my services and risk my life in sweeping clear the dangers that
threaten the state, then I have no desire to go on living!"

At the beginning of the *han-an* era [A.D. 142–43] eight men were
sent out as imperial envoys to tour the country and inspect customs and morals. All were elderly Confucians or men of prominence who had long and distinguished records of official service. Chang Kang was the only young man among them, and the
lowest in official rank. When the others had received their orders,
they set off for the outlying regions. But Chang Kang alone
buried the wheels of his carriage at the Lo-yang post station within
the capital itself, declaring, "While wolves and jackels prowl the
streets, why worry about mere foxes and wildcats!"

In time he submitted a memorial to the throne accusing the

general in chief Liang Chi and others of displaying contempt for the ruler on fifteen counts. When the memorial was presented, the entire capital quaked with fear. At this time Liang Chi's younger sister held the position of empress and the various members of the Liang family filled the court. Thus, although the emperor knew that Chang Kang was speaking the truth, he could not bring himself to act on his advice. Chang Kang held the post of governor of Kuang-ling at the time of his death.

73

屈原澤畔
Cʜ'ü Yüᴀɴ by the banks of the water

漁父江濱
Tʜᴇ ꜰɪsʜᴇʀᴍᴀɴ by the river shore

According to the *Shih chi* or *Records of the Historian,* Ch'ü Yüan, whose personal name was P'ing, was a member of the royal family of the state of Ch'u. He served as aide of the left under King Huai of Ch'u [328–299 ʙ.ᴄ.]. Possessed of wide learning and a strong will, he was wise in affairs of government and skilled in the use of words. The king put the greatest trust in him. The lord of Shang-kuan, who shared the same rank, vied with him for the king's favor and secretly envied his great ability. He thereupon began to slander his rival until the king, angered, grew cold toward Ch'ü Yüan.

Later, King Chao of the state of Ch'in invited King Huai to come to Ch'in for a meeting. "Ch'in is a nation of tigers and wolves!" warned Ch'ü Yüan. "You would do well not to make the journey!" But the king's youngest son Tzu-lan urged him to go. The king did so, and in the end died in Ch'in. His eldest son, known as King Ch'ing-hsiang, ascended the throne of Ch'u and appointed his younger brother Tzu-lan prime minister. Tzu-lan persuaded the lord of Shang-kuan to criticize Ch'ü Yüan to King Ch'ing-hsiang and the king in anger banished Ch'ü Yüan.

When Ch'ü Yüan reached the banks of the Yangtze he was one day wandering along beside the waters singing to himself, his hair unbound, his face haggard with care, his figure lean and emaciated, when a fisherman saw him and asked, "Are you not the lord of the royal family? What has brought you to this?"

Ch'ü Yüan replied, "All the world is muddied with confusion – I alone am pure! All men are drunk – I alone am sober! For this I have been banished!"

"A true sage does not quarrel with circumstance, but changes with the times," said the fisherman. "If all the world is a muddy turbulence, why do you not follow its current and rise upon its waves? If all men are drunk, why do you not drain their dregs and swill their thin wine with them? Why must you cling so tightly to this jewel of virtue and bring banishment upon your-self?"

Ch'ü Yüan replied, "I have heard it said that he who has newly washed his hair should dust off his cap, and he who has just bathed his body should shake out his robes. What man can bear to soil the cleanness of his person with the filth you call 'cir-cumstance'? Better to plunge into this never-ending current and find an end in some river fish's belly! Why should shining whiteness be soiled by the world's dust and dirt?"

Ch'ü Yüan then composed a poem in *fu* or rhyme-prose form entitled "Embracing the Sands" and, clasping a stone to his breast, cast himself into the Mi-lo River and drowned.[1]

Some hundred years later, Chia Yi, who had been appointed grand tutor to the king of Ch'ang-sha, visited the Hsiang River and cast into its waters a copy of his poem, "A Lament for Ch'ü Yüan."

1. Ch'ü Yüan is renowned as the author of the *Li sao* or "Encountering Sorrow" and other poems collected in the early anthology known as the *Ch'u Tz'u* or *Elegies of Ch'u*. The anthology has been translated by David Hawkes, *Ch'u Tzu: the Songs of the South* (London: Oxford University Press 1959).

74

于木富義

KAN MU enriches himself with righteousness

於陵辭聘

WU-LING declines the gift

According to the *Huai-nan Tzu*, Tuan-kan Mu of the state of Wei refused all offers of official position and lived in retirement at home. When Marquis Wen [424–387 B.C.], the ruler of Wei, passed by the gate of Tuan-kan Mu's hamlet, he bowed from the crossbar of his carriage in respect. His coachman said, "Tuan-kan Mu is a hemp-robed commoner. For your lordship to bow at the gate of his hamlet would seem to be rather excessive!"

Marquis Wen replied, "Tuan-kan Mu does not chase after power and profit but cherishes the way of the gentleman. Though he lives hidden away in a narrow alley, his fame spreads abroad a thousand miles. Would I dare to refrain from bowing? Tuan-kan Mu shines by the light of virtue, I shine by the light of power. Tuan-kan Mu enriches himself with righteousness, I enrich myself with wealth. Virtue is more to be honored than power, righteousness is more estimable than wealth. Tuan-kan Mu would not change places with me even if he could!"

According to the old *Lieh-nü-chuan* or *Biographies of Outstanding Women*, the king of Ch'u, having heard that Wu-ling Tzu-chung was a worthy man, wished to make him his prime minister and sent envoys bearing a gift of a hundred taels of gold to present to him.[1] Tzu-chung retired to the inner room and said to his wife, "The king wants to make me his prime minister! If I become prime minister today, tomorrow I'll ride with a team of four and strings of outriders and dine with a square yard of dishes ranged before me. Don't you think I should accept?"

His wife replied, "You earn enough to eat by weaving sandals. It's not as though you had no means to get along. You have a lute at your left hand and books at your right – plenty of joy in the midst of these. Why teams of four and strings of outriders, when all you need for comfort is a space to fit your knees into? Why a yard of dishes ranged before you at your meal, when all you need for satisfaction is one dish of meat? And yet, for the sake of a space to rest your knees in and the savor of one dish of meat you would take upon yourself the cares of the state of Ch'u – how can that be wise? These troubled times are fraught with danger. I am afraid that, worthy though you are, you will not escape with your life!"

Tzu-chung thereupon returned to the front room and conveyed to the envoys his intention of declining the offer. Eventually he and his wife ran away to another region, where they were hired by a man to water his fields.

1. The date of these events is unknown; *Mencius* III B, 10 mentions a Ch'en Chung-tzu of Wu-ling who is thought to be the same man.

FINDING LIST

NOTE: Some of the minor works cited by Hsü Tzu-kuang are now lost, unknown, or exist only in fragments.

No.	Hayakawa Text	Source	No.	Hayakawa Text	Source
1.	1.	*Chin shu* 43	16.	55.	*Chin shu* 49
	2.	*Chin shu* 35		56.	*Chin shu* 49
2.	3.	*San-kuo-chih* 35	17.	59.	*Hou Han shu* 69
	4.	*Liu t'ao* 1		60.	*Chin shu* 33
3.	9.	*Han shu* 81; *Hsi-ching tsa-chi* 2	18.	63.	*Han shu* 77
				64.	*Han shu* 45
	10.	*Ch'u-kuo hsien-hsien-chuan*	19.	65.	*Shih-shuo hsin-yü* sec. 1
4.	11.	*Shih chi* 122		66.	*Chin shu* 45
	12.	*Shih chi* 122	20.	67.	*Wei lüeh* (lost)
5.	19.	*Han shu* 54		68.	*Hou Han shu* 61
	20.	*Shih chi* 94	21.	69.	*Shih chi* 95
6.	21.	*Hou Han shu* 110		70.	*San-kuo-chih* 25
	22.	*Chin shu* 54	22.	71.	*Chin shu* 56
7.	27.	*Shih chi* 124		72.	*Shih-shuo hsin-yü* sec. 25
	28.	*Chin shu* 58	23.	83.	*Shih chi* 101
8.	33.	*Huai-nan Tzu* 17		84.	*Chin shu* 36
	34.	*Huai-nan Tzu* 17	24.	85.	*Han shu* 71
9.	37.	*Chin shu* 32		86.	*Shih chi* 54
	38.	*Tso chuan*, Duke Chao 26	25.	87.	*Huai-nan Tzu* 6
10.	39.	*Shih chi* 84		88.	Passage attributed to *Huai-nan Tzu* in *T'ai-p'ing yü-lan*, sec. on Heaven, Frost
	40.	*Chuang Tzu* 32			
11.	41.	*Shih chi* 34			
	42.	*Shih chi* 120			
12.	43.	*Chin shu* 36			
	44.	*Chin shu* 55	26.	91.	*Pei shih* 1
13.	45.	*Chin shu* 52		92.	*Shu-wang pen-chi* (fragments)
	46.	*Hou Han shu* 109	27.	93.	*Shih-chi* 103
14.	51.	*Chin shu* 1		94.	*Han Fei Tzu* sec. 13
	52.	*Shih chi* 8	28.	95.	*Han shu* 77
15.	53.	*Chin shu* 95		96.	*Chin shu* 79
	54.	*Chin shu* 34			

INDEX

NOTE: Entries in boldface type are names that appear, sometimes in abbreviated form, in Li Han's four-character phrases. Entries in caps and small caps are other names of the same persons.

179